Style
(Theory and History)

Ernest Hello

Translated By Richard Robinson

Sunny Lou Publishing Company
Portland, Oregon, USA
http://www.sunnyloupublishing.com

2nd Edition: March 17, 2024
Original Publication Date: August 4, 2021

ISBN: 978-1-955392-62-4

* * *

This translation from French is based on
the Librairie de Saint-Sulpice, Victor Palmé, Libraire-
Éditeur publication of *Le Style,* Paris, 1861.

Contents

Foreword

Sed ut perspiciatis, unde omnis iste natus error sit
voluptatem accusantium doloremque laudantium, to-
tam rem aperiam eaque ipsa, quae ab illo inventore
veritatis et quasi architecto beatae vitae dicta sunt, ex-
plicabo. Nemo enim ipsam voluptatem, quia voluptas
sit, aspernatur aut odit aut fugit, sed quia consequun-
tur magni dolores eos, qui ratione voluptatem sequi
nesciunt, neque porro quisquam est, qui dolorem ip-
sum, quia dolor sit, amet, consectetur, adipisci velit,
sed quia non numquam eius modi tempora incidunt,
ut labore et dolore magnam aliquam quaerat voluptatem. Ut enim ad minima veniam, quis nostrum ex-
ercitationemullam corporis suscipit laboriosam, nisi
ut aliquid ex ea commodi consequatur? Quis autem
vel eum iure reprehenderit, qui in ea voluptate velit
esse, quam nihil molestiae consequatur, vel illum, qui
dolorem eum fugiat, quo voluptas nulla pariatur? [33]
At vero eos et accusamus et iusto odio dignissimos
ducimus, qui blanditiis praesentium voluptatum de-
leniti atque corrupti, quos dolores et quas molestias
excepturi sint, obcaecati cupiditate non provident,
similique sunt in culpa, qui officia deserunt mollitia
animi, id est laborum et dolorum fuga. Et harum qui-
dem rerum facilis est et expedita distinctio. Nam
libero tempore, cum soluta nobis est eligendi optio,
cumque nihil impedit, quo minus id, quod maxime
placeat, facere possimus, omnis voluptas assumenda
est, omnis dolor repellendus. Temporibus autem
quibusdam et aut officiis debitis aut rerum necessitati-
bus saepe eveniet, ut et voluptates repudiandae sint et

molestiae non recusandae. Itaque earum rerum hic tenetur a sapiente delectus, ut aut reiciendis voluptatibus maiores alias consequatur aut perferendis doloribus asperiores repellat.

  – Cicero, 45 BC (*de Finibus Bonorum et Malorum*)

Preface

The law of Art is the law of Life.

Such is the thinking of the book I offer to the public today.

Error, which, by habitude or by nature, divides men and things, has presented human speech as a game whose rules are foreign to the laws of life and independent of the nature of things.

I have wanted, in this book, which presents a very rigorous unity of thought, although its chapters may not seem to cohere, I have wanted to study human speech in some of its laws and some of its errors, to study it in itself and sketch out rapidly some traits of its history, so as to spare young men the circuitous routes they nearly all go in, and to show them in advance, before their thinking has gone astray, the straight line that leads to knowledge of human speech and the intelligence of its history.

– Ernest Hello

Style

Style is a power that, like all powers, has need of being avenged. That word, which represents so great a thing, is one of the most dishonored words in the world. That association of ideas that I have often spoken of, and that I speak of again today, has given us the habitude of considering style as the art of stitching words together one after the other, the art of arranging phrases with an empty symmetry, both elegant and insignificant. For rhetors, style, like all beautiful things almost, style is a negative thing: according to their thinking, it has to do, in order to write well, with avoiding a multitude of inconveniences, locutions that are not *noble*, expressions that are too familiar, words that grate on the ear, and when one has achieved those mechanical conditions, which resemble, by their multiplicity and their inaneness, the conditions of a game, *one knows how to write*, and one earns the first-place prize.

In order to judge writers from this point of view, and rank them, there would need to be a way to count their faults, as in secondary school. The boy with the least number of faults would be proclaimed as coming in first. This procedure would have the merit of being a confession. It would confess our secret thought; it would confess that we consider absolute abstention like perfection, and that, for us, he who did nothing is he who did best.

The style that rhetors love and recommend is made in the image of nothingness. If someone thinks, that shocks them doubtless quite a bit; but if someone speaks, that shocks them even more. What they don't pardon, in style, is precision and affirmation. What they admire in it is its vagueness and impersonality. Their counsels, or, as they say, their rules, could be summed up like this:

"In general, to be really wise, one must think nothing, believe nothing, hope for nothing, love nothing, hate nothing, for thought, faith, hope, and love all shock certain people who must not be shocked. Keep your mind in the lukewarm atmosphere of doubt and boredom. Bore your readers a lot, as much as you bore yourself if possible. Bore them, bore them I say! it is the way to appear reasonable to them. Anything that does not bore them seems *exaggerated* to them. So believe nothing; in that way you are sure never to love anything, and if you should love something, one might say that you have some exaltation. All the same, as one must not take things too far, even in nothingness, although that might be the best route, – I admit, young pupils, I admit the hypothesis wherein, carried away by the inexperienced ardor of your age, you feel yourselves drawn more towards one opinion than its opposite. I hope, for your sake, that this misfortune rarely happens. But you must be prepared for every eventuality, even that wherein temptation might make you believe something. It's a strange case: but man is weak, we are not perfect. By admitting then the temptation to believe something, the duty of a good writer is to dissimulate it, as much as possible. To avoid affirmation, one must have recourse to those happy artifices that rhetoric teaches: one must say: *perhaps, it seems, it is permitted to express oneself thus*.

"Thought is already quite odious as it is. If, by some unhappy circumstance, you have one, you must destroy it at the very least, as much as possible, with the help of speech, which was given to you but with that end in mind. If you have a thought, you are thereby suspected of originality even. If you went even further to express it with energy or courage, you should enter completely into the category of fools. Ah! if you have a thought, at least throw a veil over that shame, and that veil is speech. If your style, effaced and dead, resembles everyone else's, you will be pardoned perhaps for the impropriety of possessing an idea. Efface then all that could be tall, broad, deep: efface everything that, in your speech, might clearly reveal your thinking and your soul, and your character and your person; make those phrases long, balanced, anodyne and impersonal, which have been read everywhere, before having been read once again in your pages.

"Resemble everyone, and even if you have the misfortune of saying something, still pretend to say nothing: for speech has been given to man to dissimulate his thought, not even by a bold negation, but by means of a long, trailing, and elegant veil."

That's how Rhetoric speaks. That's how, at least, it would speak if it dared to speak. But it does not even have the courage to say that it does not have the courage; it does not even have the strength to sense its feebleness. It does not see far enough into itself to perceive its nullity.

It has the practice of Nothingness alright. But it does not have enough intelligence to have the theory. It does not know itself any more than it knows some other thing. It ignores its own formula. I have just presented it to it. While looking at it, it will not recognize it. It will find it exaggerated; to correct it, it will dissimulate under *perhaps* and *nearly*. Whereby, it will prove me right better than I can prove myself right. Because I can give only the formula of Nothingness. It would know how to set the example and offer the practice. By softening, through a thousand restrictions, the coarseness of words that are much more precise than I attribute to it, it would absolutely demonstrate its truth and exactitude. For if it pronounced them word by word, it would understand them, and thereby it would give the lie to them even, as it would be saying something.

Let's forget rhetoric for now. It can be useful one moment, because by preaching falsity it inspires horror sometimes, and sets out, in that fashion, down the road to truth. But let's forget rhetoric for now.

What is style?

Style is human speech. Human speech must be frank and discreet: to combine those two words in one word, it must be true.

Truth, which is the law of thought and the law of life, is also the law of speech and is always the same truth.

Error, which divides everything, has found the means to give a certain direction to thought, another to life, a third to speech, to invent diverse and contradictory rules for all those things.

Let's wake up. Open our eyes. Notice the simplest and most unnoticed things, the Unity of the law.

Truth is life. It is clear that man must live in truth.

It is clear that man's thought must conform to the same truth as his action, so that there are not two contradictory truths.

It is equally clear that man's speech must conform to the same truth as his thought and his action, so that there are not three contradictory truths.

So man must:

Live in truth;

Think as he lives;

And speak as he thinks.

That is the law of style. We are now at total simplicity, because we are at total truth.

Is that to say that every man's style will need to resemble each other's?

No; for if the truth is one, we are diverse amongst ourselves, and the impressions we receive from it are always diverse, without their ever being contradictory.

The same sun makes lilies blossom and roses bloom. Lilies and roses assimilate the same light and the same heat differently, because their abilities, their needs, their internal aptitudes, differ without contradicting each other.

In the reign of error, men contradict themselves and resemble one another. They do not have style, because their characters are effaced, and they dispute amongst themselves in error and at cross purposes, without understanding one another, without refuting one another, without persuading one another.

Error is monotonous and contradictory. Truth is one and always novel. It leaves to each man his style.

The ideas that a man expresses are everyone's property. But that man's style is his particular property.

Put the same words in the mouth of two men, those two words will not have the same sound.

One man speaks: the sonorous sphere that surrounds him is wide; the vibrations of his voice echo in the intelligible world, he opens a window onto the infinite.

Another man speaks: he articulates the same syllables; the sonorous sphere that surrounds him is narrow, and his voice does not carry. You have caught a glimpse of nothing beyond the immediate sense of the words that he will have pronounced.

Style is the explosion of our person: it is our creation. The idea that we express, we do not create it.

But we create our style: a man can, without being a genius, see a great truth. But to say it, that truth, in definitive terms, to tell it in an immortal language, to sign it with his name, to associate it, in the eyes of the human race, with that signature, one needs be a man of genius. The location of genius, it is style: style is his residence, his proof, his mark and his glory. Whatever you say, if it is style you lack, you will not have glory.

Style cannot be replaced by thought, no matter how splendid one might suppose it. Nothing dispenses with it. It is the condition of glory; like it, to be deserved, and like it, to be conquered. We say of a man that he possesses a language, when he finally speaks it as he wishes to speak it. The fact is that language, and above all the French language, is not free for the taking by the first Tom, Dick or Harry to stroll along: it requires a fight and surrenders only to the person who dominates it. Humanity, which is so difficult for the thinker, does not consent finally to admire him except when he knows how to compel, by splendorous speech, its recalcitrant admiration. It is bent by force under the whip of speech, and seems to say in spite of itself, in reference to the great writer who struggled against his idea to seize it, against language in order to dominate it:

> *Let him reign brilliantly over his conquest,*
> *And let him crown his head with his victory!*

When a man has conquered his style, he loses, like sovereigns, the pleasure of incognito. One recognizes him from the moment he speaks. He betrays himself from the moment he appears.

Rhetoric advises us to imitate great writers. It believes they have a recipe and that it suffices to follow it. Their recipe? – to be oneself. Their person is inviolable, and no one can appropriate it. All that one can do is to steal their habit, and here is the robber's punishment: the stolen habit does not fit, it is a size too big for him.

Give a man the ideas of another man: give them all to him: the plan of some work of art, in its entirety, and the details, the materials, everything, even the words, – the two works of art will never resemble each other.

The great writer and *the other* will be separated by an abyss, eternally. Each one of them will have his own style. Style! there it is again, that great word, the secret. But what is the meaning of that word? What is style, after all?

The same idea, penetrating a thousand intelligences, will emerge in a thousand different expressions. Those expressions will vary as will vary the resultant secret work that the idea will have had in each of us. Our expression will result from the elaboration that the idea will have subjected our soul to. The idea will give our speech the aspect it will have taken in us. Absorbed by us, it will enter our mould, fashion itself there, and speak, while it manifests itself on the outside, the expression that our particular intelligence will have given to it. The relation established between it and us will be manifested by our speech. Our style, it is the signature of our person affixed to an idea; our style, it is our coat of arms; it is our imprint, our effigy, our crown, struck onto the warm metal, onto the metal that is still in fusion.

The same law exists everywhere; it is the law of the universe. It is the unity that gives to bodies their beauty. Beauty, beating money out of matter, imprints the royal effigy on that inert and indifferent mass.

The style of a writer and that of a rhetor will differ then, just like the dog rose that stands out on the bush differs from the imitation in paper that one can make.

The first will be organic, the second mechanical.

Organic style, it is the living word at the service of a living idea. Mechanical style, it is an arrangement of words made for the benefit of certain conventions. Organic style goes to the heart of things and cuts to the quick; mechanical style slips to the side of them; one could say that it is afraid to speak, because of a bad conscience. The first is free, frank, determined, bold; it is fearless, because it is without reproach. The second is timid, false, indecisive, cowardly and a liar. The first is essentially personal; it requires that man think, and speak as he thinks; that he actually believe, intimately, vivaciously, all that he says. The second gleans from all sides some withered flowers that have already served a thousand times; it is composed of old rags. The first so closely grips the thought that it makes a single body with it. You cannot detach them, to admire one without the other and to think the same idea without using the words that it seems to have chosen to express itself in. The second is a loose and flowing piece of drapery that flutters around the thought without ever touching it. The first is a battle, the second a heated exchange. I call the first organic, because it issues alive from the idea, like a flower issues from a seed; its beauty is the shining exterior of an interior beauty that it reveals to us; it knows how to make stand out, in relief, in evidence, all aspects of thought; it makes latent splendors shine; it shows the light of the word everywhere; it sets the powder keg on fire, so that the detonation and flames will waken those who are asleep.

I call the second mechanical, because it is artificially produced by exterior elements and juxtaposed pieces; its elegance is miserable, for it is borrowed: it does not belong to it, it comes from without. There exists between those two styles the same difference that exists between a living man and an automaton. Organic style has allures all its own; it has roughness and ardors, it has unexpected, varied, spontaneous movements like life; it changes expression like the human physiognomy that it is; it is lively and penetrating like fire and like a glance. Mechanical style has the stiff and clumsy movements of a machine.

It has no grace, because it has no force; it is immobile, and if it seems to move, that movement is colder than its immobility. One senses the intention of the mechanic who would like, at moments, to warm it, and who, not having any warmth at his disposal, operates a spring-loaded mechanism.

Mechanical style is sometimes elegant, in the false sense of the word.

Organic style is always simple; but its simplicity has the permission to resemble that of lightning, when two electrical clouds bump into each other in space on a stormy day.

Mechanical style is sentimental, penetrated by that silly and false unction that seems made for chanting the psalms of commonplaces. The sentimental tone uncovers the bottom of the speaker's soul, in other words, his most profound insensibility.

Organic style is full, solid, and chaste, both expansive and contained at the same time. It brings with it that modesty of great thoughts and profound emotions that, as calm as they are ardent, have some discretion even in their splendor: it has the integrity of hard bodies that have fire hidden in their veins. The fire is the great purifier (πυρ, in Greek, fire). That kind of style, it has passed through fire; it is a rock, it is a diamond.

Mechanical style is flabbiness and viscous.

If the advice of rhetoric, the advice to imitate great writers, or those it calls great, is ridiculous advice, the advice of assimilating them would be serious advice. It can happen, in fact, that by plunging into the genius of a great man, you will be penetrated, impregnated by him; that something from him passes into you, on condition that, nevertheless, you merit it and that you present a penetrable surface to his rays. That cannot be done by copying, by the discovery of a procedure, but by an intimate communication of warmth and life. Man is not nourished, like animals of inferior race, by juxtaposition; they are nourished by assimilation. Now, the writer gives his style, that is to say his speech, that is to say himself. It is permitted to be nourished on that.

I have tried to describe, in a general way, what a man's style is.

I will try to given an account of what men's style has been.

Let's cast an eye on writers; they can be classified into three categories.

There are, among them, the class of children. The man-child sees himself and looks around; he is surprised, he admires; he is surprised by everything, he admires everything. He contemplates while speaking and acting, with a naïve stupefaction, and an infantile joy. He does not yet think about speaking better or acting better. He takes pleasure in what he is, like a child with his first plaything. He looks around himself. He finds that the light is beautiful, and he says so. He looks at matter, and he paints it with his words; he paints it, and that's it. He does not think clearly about the kind of rapport he can have with it: he loves things for themselves. The poet-child has Homer for his type. Homer is a far ways off from being the ideal of human genius. If antiquity had not surpassed him, it is because it always imitated him, and imitation forbids superiority. No copy surpasses its model. Man can surpass Homer and surpass him immensely; but Homer remains an immortal child. The characteristic epithets that have adopted his name, the Homeric epithets, so shocking in each translation, are explained by the poet's age, by the

character of childhood. Homer looks much more than
he reflects. He looks at his Achilles, and as the swift-
ness of his feet is a visible quality, striking to a
child's eye, he associates that quality, from then on,
to the idea of Achilles indissolubly, and Achilles will
always be for him the swift-footed Achilles. If we
should show him wounded, if we should show him
paralyzed, he would still call him the swift-footed
Achilles, just as he calls Jupiter *wise*, even when he
shows him to be duped, mocked, deceived, insane.
The Homeric epithet does not originate from a reflection made at the moment it is expressed. It results
from an ancient observation made once and for all, on
a day when Achilles was running. Homer is the poet
of observation. He marvels and does not question. He
effaces himself before his objects, in order to describe
for us what they are. Homer entering into life is like a
child arriving in Paris. He looks at the houses one after the other, not to judge them, not to classify them
nor to choose one, but to look at them. One is white,
another is gray; this one is low, that one is tall. Later,
he will climb the towers of Notre-Dame, and he will
look at the city. Then he will orient himself. He will
learn how to go from one place to another. While
waiting, he walks around. The child never goes anywhere. For him, the route is already an end in itself.
He walks around endlessly. That is why Homer goes
on at such great length. He takes so much pleasure
looking at a shield, that he stops before that curious
object, without paying attention to the time. We can
now interpret Homer, and show how all Greek poetry
is nothing but his daughter. I have already spoken
elsewhere a few words on this same subject; but he

cannot interpret; he looks and he paints.

But one grows old quickly, and Homer does not last forever. The child would admire the glitter of gold; the man desires now to possess gold. The pleasure of the eyes no longer suffices. Humanity will change styles: the child was a colorist, the man will be an observer. The child looked at objects to see them, the man will look at them to put them to use. The child did not relate them to anything, the man relates them to himself. That return to himself will profoundly modify his manner of speaking. Earlier, he spoke in order to paint; now he will speak in order to speak well. There you have it, for those who will listen. His speech is no longer the spontaneous expression of his joy or his distress; it is no longer a cry or a song; it is a literary composition. Earlier, he saw in nature a scene to be contemplated; now he will see a field to exploit; and, as he thinks of himself when he examines, he thinks of himself when he speaks. Homer will make way for Virgil. Unfortunately, man, taken with the beauties of the child, will try to imitate him. That is why the Homeric epithet, acceptable in Homer, is ridiculous in Virgil; this is because Homer lets its slip in without it being noticed, while Virgil, listening and measuring with the greatest attention to all the syllables that he pronounces, when he says a word, he does it expressly. If Homer is given a pass on so many things, it is because children are not held accountable. If Virgil elicits sensitivity, it is because he is a man of the world. He is not a child, he is not a friend either; he is a man of the world and a man of affairs who did his toilette before speaking to you, and who finds pleasure in the melody of his words.

He has neither enough inexperience, nor enough experience, to forget himself while speaking to you. He
is no longer a child, and he is not mature. He has un-
learnt abandonment, and he has not yet relearnt it. We
love the swift-footed Achilles, and we do not love the
pious Aeneas; it is because Achilles acts *in good faith*
in his rapidity, and Aeneas does not in his piety.
Ulysses seeks Ithaca, in order to see again the smoke
that rises in the evening above the thatch roofs. Aeneas is led to Italy by religious and political consider-
ations that he does not seem to understand. He is not
serious or moved; he has the serious attitude of a sim-
pleton.

His piety, like the bravery of Gias or Cloanthe
(*fortemque Giam, fortemque Cloanthum*), appeared at
critical moments, demanded by the measure of the
verse. But the author himself seems to treat it lightly.
We notice that the Homeric epithet revolves, almost
always in Homer, around an external quality that is
really there where one observes it; in Virgil, it revolves around a moral quality which the author does
not seem to believe in: Homer saw Achilles run. But
if Aeneas was pious, if Cloanthe was brave, Virgil ap-
parently knows nothing about it, and the more he repeats it, the less he seems to know about it.

The critics, while admiring Virgil, seem to attribute the decadence that succeeded him to the very
excess of his perfection. They seem to think that after
him humanity fell because it could not keep itself up
for long at such heights. That view is shallow. If
decadence followed Virgil, it is, I believe, not in spite
of him, but because of him. If it developed after him,

it is because he planted the seed.

In terms of style, the seed is decadence; it is the cult of the word sought after for itself. It was Virgil's hability to hide that seed of death under the flowers he had at his disposal; but it is still there, without having suffocated it. The feelings of nature, tenderness, and melancholy in his soul made a real finery for Virgil: Nisus and Euryale, Mezentius and his horse, are all there to attest to it. But the false finery, the cult of the phrase, was always there. Now, false criticism always admires the writer's defects and forgets his qualities. It is the defects of other men that it puts forward for imitation; and as, in fact, defects are much more imitable than positive qualities, it is on the former, and not the latter, that his imitators rely. They did not come away from Virgil with that sweet and tender feeling for the countryside; they could not hear, as he could, the steers' mooing; they were unable to appreciate, unlike him, the gentle soughing of the trees that were asleep; but they knew how to imitate the mechanical construction of Virgilian verse. From there the decadence, that is to say the idolatry of the phrase.

Ovid complained about being a stranger among barbarians, because alone in the midst of them he spoke a language all his own. I believe that Ovid was boasting. He acted misunderstood, but I am certain that fundamentally those barbarians understood him and loved him. What is even more contrary to barbarism is simplicity; what is more conformant with barbarism is affectation. Affectation ought to make savages rejoice; they are savages only by dint of not being simple. Ovid had lowered poetry to the level of a play on words. In an intelligent and knowledgeable society, that is to say a simple one, he would have really been misunderstood, and really mocked. They would have shown him the door, and they would have done it forcibly. Among the barbarians, there was a public worthy of him: the applause must not have been lacking.

We have seen, in Homer, the man-child naively loving and joyously celebrating things and words; we have seen, in Virgil, the man, having outgrown childhood, but still far from maturity, loving with research and celebrating with ostentation, as a means to fortune and glory, things and words.

What will the mature man do then?

The child, in the face of things and words, reported on them as he found them, for what they were. The young man, in the face of things and words, exploited them, related them to himself.

The mature man, in the face of things and words, will report on them in terms of the thought they must serve, the thought they must express.

Standing before a sea vessel, Homer admired the exterior arrangement of the boat, Virgil thought of Aeneas and the political consequences of the voyage; the *third* man would think of a great voyage and a great arrival.

The first style has a character of enthusiasm to it; the second style has a character of research to it; the third style has a character of forgetfulness to it. It is to this latter style then that it belongs to resplend and shine.

Great style, the only style allowed going forward, forgets; by consequence it finds itself and it contains itself. Sovereign beauty refuses to give itself to the man who makes light of it, it gives itself to whomever arms himself with it. It refuses to give itself to the man who wants to makes a trophy of it, it abandons itself to whomever wants to make use of it.

One claims that it has caprices. I believe that that is the law of its caprices.

I hear your objection. You do not wish to consider among writers, then, you are going to tell me, any other than great writers? You admit only the first class? You count only what is sublime?

Pardon me. That so-simple law of simplicity, that obligation to speak in order to tell, and not in order to speak, is true on all rungs of the intellectual ladder.

Plato knew it at certain moments (when he is a sophist, which is, alas! all too often, he totally forgot it); sophists are rhetors of philosophy. Sophistic Plato abandons the category of mature men in order to enter into that of young men.

Tacitus speaks in order to express his thought. His speech is simple, strong, and brief. Everything that is strong is brief. Tacitus has given to the Latin language an energy that, without him, it would never have known. It suffices to think of Cicero, who is the Ovid of prose and the epitome of the rhetor, in order to appreciate Tacitus, while measuring with the eye the distance that separates them. For Cicero, everything is abstract. Rome, it is the republic, the city, the State. For Tacitus, everything is alive: he calls people by their names. He almost always has the contained vigor of great anger, and sometimes the serene vigor of great justices. That man's style reveals to me the capacity in him to remain quiet, particular characteristic of men who sense posterity behind them and who charge it with their vengeance. In great style, silence always plays a large part in it. There is silence in Tacitus' style. Vulgar anger bursts out, petty anger prattles; but there is an indignation that feels the need to remain quiet, as if to let things speak for themselves, while waiting for the justice of the future. Tacitus is not only the greatest writer of the Latin language, he is the greatest writer of classical antiquity.

It is impossible, when speaking of style, not to cite Bossuet.[1] The particular character of his speech is to make present the facts that he recounts. One has greatly admired in the funeral oration for Henrietta of England the famous exclamation: "O terrible night, etc." where, like a thunderclap, that surprising news resounds: "Madame dies! Madame is dead!"[2]

But I do not believe anyone has discovered

---

[1]Bossuet: Jacques-Bénigne Bossuet (1627-1704), a French bishop and theologian at the time of Louis XIV.

[2]Funeral oration: "O nuit désastreuse! ô nuit effroyable, où retentit tout à coup, comme un éclat de tonnerre, cette étonnante nouvelle: MADAME se meurt, MADAME est morte!" *Oraisons Funèbres*, Bossuet. In English translation: "O disastrous night! o terrible night, when all of a sudden, like a thunderclap, that surprising news resounds: MADAME dies, MADAME is dead!"

where the beauty of that phrase lies; it is not in the exclamation, it is entirely in the word "surprising." That
there is the thunderclap. Change that one word, and
nothing remains; why? Because it is Bossuet's surprise that makes the present catastrophe real for us.

It transports us into total darkness, into the
night of the thunderclap. Bossuet, the funeral orator
of great men, is surprised with a voluntary naïvety by
the coffin that lies before him. One could say that he,
Bossuet himself, cannot get used to the thought that it
expresses. Bossuet climbs up to the pulpit to speak of
death, and, all of a sudden, terrified as if he was looking at it squarely in the face for the first time, in the
pulpit of Notre-Dame, Bossuet is surprised by death.

Nor can I fail to mention De Maistre: there are
names that impose themselves on us. I cannot say everything today; I will point out between those two
glories of France, Bossuet and De Maistre, a very
striking contrast that nobody has thought of.

Bossuet lays out his thought slowly, seriously,
royally, like a purple mantle; De Maistre clenches his.

Bossuet expresses only one thought at a time,
and takes it for a stroll on high, isolated, exposed to
looks from earth. He takes in hand the misery of human things in order to give a long spectacle of it to
men. He makes one drink the chalice to the lees. He
continually repeats, and never does he not repeat. He
always says the same thing, and he never says too
much. He consecrates commonplaces, and when he
says for the hundred thousandth time that man is mortal, his booming voice gives us the impression that we

just heard it for the first time.

De Maistre does precisely the opposite, not by method, but naturally.

He groups a certain number of thoughts together, which do not always seem to go together, and he binds them in the same phrase, one against the other. Surprised to be found together, they are seen with a strange air, which gives them a new aspect in our eyes.

In an idea that he would express for the first time, Bossuet would show the old view of it. In an idea that he would express for the thousandth time, De Maistre would give evidence of a new aspect to it, or so it would seem. De Maistre always seems like he is expressing a paradox; Bossuet always seems like he is expressing a commonplace.

De Maistre *seeks without affectation* great effects in style or, if you will, finds them, and does not seek them.

Bossuet absolutely disdains everything that might resemble an intention.

When brilliance comes to him, he has an attitude, while accepting it, of complaisance.

De Maistre has habitually legitimate traits, Bossuet has no traits whatsoever. The periodic is the natural form of that style which is too proud to be chopped up, too ample ever to be sharpened.

Notice that I bring those two men together here only from the point of view of style. I have not spoken about their gaze. De Maistre has the more piercing view.

De Maistre rejuvenates the thought that he expresses; Bossuet disdains to rejuvenate it; he gives it as it is, armed with its old age, decked with the ages it has traversed before arriving finally at him in order to be repeated once again.

The law of simplicity, as I said earlier, obliges at every rung on the intellectual ladder. I will give an example of it.

Let's find a man who has never lived in the world of ideas, who has never received a thought, not first hand, or second hand, who has absolutely not received one; who is ignorant of Beauty; who has never lifted his head, who is not a poet, in the great acceptation of the word, who has only spoken very small things, already spoken by others before him, so that any small merit of invention does not belong to him, a man however who makes himself read and who does not allow himself to be forgotten.

That man exists; his name is La Fontaine.

That man, who has never had an inkling of anything great, and who has not even imagined the small things that he has told us about, has in particular and curiously but one merit, one alone, nothing but one, and that strangely attests to the power of that unique quality by which he lives, he who had so many reasons not to live.

That power that immortalizes La Fontaine, it is style.

All praise for him is contained in that one word, and, if anyone wants to praise him, it is absolutely impossible to add a second word.

He knew how to tell a story, he knew how to write. O French language! what power is at your disposal then that La Fontaine should be famous?

I do not believe that La Fontaine had, in his passage here on earth, ever cast a glance at heaven; I do not believe that he had ever felt for one instant the torment or joy of eternal things. I do not believe that it is possible to perceive, to seize, to suspect, to divine, by inspecting that dead heart of his, where finally the place of God resided in him. I do not believe that it is possible, on listening to him, to detect a cry, nor that he had felt, with respect to whatever it might be, before conversion, an aspiration.

"My burden, it is my love," said a man whose name I hardly dare pronounce on so insignificant an occasion: it renders too much honor to La Fontaine to have Saint Augustine intervene on his behalf. However, the truth is the truth, with respect to everything, *maxima in minimis*. To which side then does La Fontaine lean? Does he love a true or a false beauty, or only the appearance of beauty? No. Some are attracted to greatness but do not know where it lies; they give witness consequently to a native elevation that eludes them. La Fontaine is not one of them.

He desires neither true greatness nor false greatness, he does not suspect the existence of the sublime. He retains not admiration, – his class of men do not admire, – but praise for the hability that is had from business concerns. He has a partiality for wiliness! horrible thing!

His ideal, it is the fox!

I do not insist on the *thinker* and the *poet*. It is all there in that phrase: his ideal, it is the fox. Let's talk about the writer.

Is he a writer? Alas! yes: I'm upset.

There where elevation is missing, I would have everything be missing. I prefer absent gifts to betrayed gifts. But the critic's duty is to take everything into account. He must conciliate the enthusiasm given to great things and the attention given to small things. His glory is to love and assist what soars; but that glorious love does not exclude taking into account the pace of those who walk on the ground. Love never refuses to stoop.

The man who does not admire is never admirable. We will *not admire* La Fontaine then. The critic must reserve his solemn words for men and things that are admirable. There are those who have dared speak of the *genius* of La Fontaine.

That profanation of great words is more fatal than one might suppose. It takes away men's respect from really great things. It compromises real majesties, by saluting in their name those who do not wear the crown. No, La Fontaine should not be admired, but praised, appreciated, enjoyed to the degree that he merits.

Without style, who would he be like? He

would be like Florian. Let's look then into the characteristics of that style, which has had the strength of drawing such a line of demarcation.

One characteristic is frankness. Florian does not believe in the individuals he puts on stage, La Fontaine believes in his. Florian tries to make them speak. La Fontaine puts himself in their shoes and speaks through their mouth.

He makes himself into a rabbit, and a rabbit in good faith! That's his secret. It is not enough for a man, but it is something. And because he acts in good faith, he never exaggerates. If Perrette did not act in good faith, she would exaggerate the pig whose birth she predicts. Exaggeration is the lie of honest men, Joseph de Maistre said. But La Fontaine and Perrette act in good faith.

It was, when I had it, of reasonable *size.*

Reasonable is marvelous! Perrette has evidently a clear and actual view of that pig; but she would wake up from that sleep if she pushed it too far. She introduces wisdom into that dream, in order to introduce some verisimilitude.

La Fontaine raised himself one day above himself. One day he attained beauty; on that day then, he wrote *The Oak and the Reed*. Then, and only then perhaps, he raised himself to the conception of one of the great laws of universal order: he appeared to see weakness in the strong: he didn't see it from on high, as that would have made him stop being himself, but he caught a glimpse of it.

He had the glory of suspecting that every creature, at the moment when it says to itself "I am
strong," will be struck dead. And what language was
that of the oak! Suddenly the stupidity of pride appears! As it offers its protection with imbecilic em-
phasis and diffuses the powerlessness that loves to
boast! As it realizes that it will protect no one, that it
would have need of protection itself, and that it desires neither to protect, for it is not good, nor to be
protected, for it thinks itself strong! As its ruin is an-
ticipated! As it is contained in the first phrase it pronounces!

You really do have reason to accuse nature.

La Fontaine tells us only about the oak's
strength, and makes us think only of its weakness; he
makes it speak like a sovereign, and we sense the
condemned being so strongly in it that the catastrophe
has already arrived, for the reader, before the author
has had a chance to see it. The reed is also as precise
and brief in its response as the oak was long-winded
and oratorical:

I bend and do not break.
But let's wait and see.

There you have it: the language of him who
will be right.

In general, La Fontaine is dry; also, with him,
the traits of feeling take on a value all their own. They
are moreover of an exquisite delicateness.

When two pigeons reunite, La Fontaine leaves

it for us to judge:

> *By so many pleasures, they paid for their troubles.*

Their troubles! only one of them has traveled however. La Fontaine believes, in good faith, that they have shared the same perils. He can no longer distinguish the one who loves from the one who is loved.

Those charming words have this in particular and deliciously going for them – that it is easy, on reading them, to feel them vaguely, to feel their effect without bothering to notice them. La Fontaine appears not to perceive it, and invites the reader to do as he does. His literary insouciance is his charm in our eyes. He does not pretend, he does not seek, he does not even find; he encounters. And we thank him all the more for his simplicity, when we remind ourselves, on seeing him, of his date of birth. We see him as fully contained within the seventeenth century. So the least naïvety becomes a surprising merit. Change La Fontaine's century, and you will no longer find yourself the same with respect to him, even though he will always be the same with respect to you.

His title [to renown], in our eyes, when we think about it and even when we do not think about it, is to have resisted the air he breathed, and to have been La Fontaine even though Boileau was around.

To La Fontaine's credit, I add also that he has a sense of justice. I'm not talking about superior justice: that touches on mystery, and he would need, in order to conjecture it, to lift his eyes to there where the fabulist's view does not go. I am speaking about justice that is a bit gross, a bit bourgeois, but real and respectable, what good common sense perceives, about *visible* justice, in a word. That there is what dictated the *Wolf and the Lamb*.

It would not be impossible unfortunately to surprise La Fontaine red-handed in a contradiction and to encounter him sometimes among the partisans of the wolf and the assassins of the lamb. His God is, after all, I will not say power (that idea is too lofty for him), but *know-how*.

This is so true that I take up *The Oak and the Reed* again, and in spite of myself I add the following reflection. If La Fontaine condemns the oak, it is not because it is proud or mean, it is because it is going to perish. Instead of saying: It is wrong, it boasts, therefore it will perish. La Fontaine says: It will perish, therefore it is wrong.

Because of this, we can never praise in him anything fully but style. Those of you who love the truth, and who think on it, arm yourselves then with style, ally yourselves with that power, and when you have, like La Fontaine, mastered speech, know how to make use of it as La Fontaine did not.

A fable, if I'm not mistaken, could have great destinies. There is a glory that would be all its own, there is a language that would be suitable for it. What would be the condition? It would need to interrogate the nature of things and understand this word: symbolism.

It would adorn itself this very moment with the dignity that it lacks. It would quit the domain of pastimes and enter the domain of art.

A sense of symbolism is absolutely lacking in La Fontaine.

He puts animals and vegetables on the scene, but I don't get a feeling of nature from him.

The countryside is absent from his work, as is thought, as is beauty.

A fabulist's most elevated characteristic would be a respect for types. That characteristic is completely and absolutely lacking in La Fontaine. What lions are like his lions, and what eagles like his eagles! My how his pettiness stands out when the ac- tors of his dramas bear great names! I have told you, he is at ease only in the company of foxes. I do not believe that he has ever awakened in any man that feeling of human greatness which is one of the joys and glories of art!

I cannot keep myself from making a remark here that is striking and so obvious that it is not worth mentioning. La Fontaine puts individuals onto the scene who all act *crafty*, and one dares to speak of art with respect to him! Have men not yet noticed then that the opposite of art is craftiness? One has really got to be quite old not to have noticed that yet.

M. Taine has published some articles on La Fontaine in the *Journal des Débats*. M. Taine wishes to inspire us with the most vivid admiration for the fabulist; he has succeeded in provoking the profoundest disdain for his hero; but La Fontaine will forgive him, for if M. Taine has blackened his reputation, he hasn't noticed it.

"Our Champenois," he says, "suffers quite a bit when sheep are eaten by wolves, and when sots are duped by knaves... Also, his maxims have nothing of the heroic about them... his most generous are to obey, to accept evil for what it is, for it is a part of the human condition. He would never have been an Alceste; I do not even know if he would have been a Philinte.[3] He counsels rather crudely flattery and base flattery. The stag puts the queen who had previously strangled his wife and son on the same level as the gods and celebrates her like a court poet. La Fontaine approves of perfidy, and when the trick is profitable and well played, he forgets that it is an ambush.

"He represents a wise man who, pursued by a fool, flatters him with pretty, lying speech, and ever so mawkishly breaks his spine and knocks him senseless. He finds the invention good, and he counsels us to practice it."

The same M. Taine, in the same work, says the following when speaking about the same man:

"He is a *poet*. I believe that, of all the French, he is the most veritably that has ever been."

That's how, with M. Taine, the association of ideas goes. He is the one who has the modesty to inform us which acceptation of the word poet he takes.

---

[3]Alceste... Philinte: both are characters in Molière's comedy, *Le Misanthrope*.

M. Taine continues:

"More than anyone else he had two great traits: the faculty of forgetting the real world and that of living in the *ideal* world; the gift of not seeing things in their true light, and that of following internally his beautiful dreams."

Was it that ideal world that La Fontaine was walking in when he counseled *base flattery*? That man had, so far as it appears, a rather novel conception of the ideal world. And in his beautiful dreams, do you know what he dreamt of? He dreamt of *well-played tricks*. What a poet!

Also, M. Taine declares that he was *enthusiastic*:

"Even when he made naughty remarks, he refrained from any gross word; he kept the style of good company."

Let's look at that enthusiasm a bit!

It is clearly with that same enthusiasm that La Fontaine must have *not seen things in their true light*.

It is true that that same critic, speaking of the same writer, admires him one instant later as an *observer* and insists at length on that new praise. He forgets that La Fontaine does not see things in their true light, and shows him to us "as an attentive and curious stranger before the living world that was established in him."

What to say? M. Taine's enthusiasm prevents him from perceiving the contradictions that are met

with under his quill. He does not see them, because he
is enthusiastic and because they are true.

M. Taine believes that La Fontaine is a connoisseur of men. He sees him as a representative of
France. He would send La Fontaine's works to
whomever wished to get familiar with them.

In the name of humanity and in the name of
France, I believe that every man and every Frenchman is allowed to respond to that: No, the man whom
La Fontaine depicts, it is man such as M. Taine conceives of him, but that is not man; it is not the man
created in God's image, the man redeemed by the Son
of God, it is not even the fallen man. La Fontaine has
not seen the precipice's depth; it is the exterior enve-
lope of the fallen man, it is his imperfectly-drawn sil-
houette.

The France that La Fontaine represents, it is
the France, in so far as it appears, that M. Taine conceives of; it is not France as it truly is, as it appears
when, giving an account of itself in history, it opens
the book of its life to the first page and shows us these
words: *Gesta Dei per Francos*.

You have not heard anything yet: it gets better. M. Taine gives himself away somewhere. He
wrote a word that is his last word, a word that sums
him up; he gave away his secret. He says (ah! I
wouldn't dare put words in his mouth, it is much better if I cite him), he says that La Fontaine *takes the
sadness out of truth*.

The truth, such as M. Taine conceives of it, is

sad; and, as far as La Fontaine is concerned, it appears to be happy.

I owe M. Taine some thanks: his formula has helped me to find the true formula. To say everything about La Fontaine in a single word, to summarize my accusation against him, I have only one word to change in M. Taine's phrase: I merely have to say it:

La Fontaine takes the joy out of truth.

To demonstrate the power of style, I have chosen La Fontaine, in order to show that power acting all on its own (as much as possible), isolated, and on the lowest rungs of the intellectual ladder. I wanted to show how posterity loves those who knew how to write. But why? The love of style for us, I believe, stems from our love of life. Provided that the soul shines, shows itself, reveals to us something of its interior life, we accept that cry without dispute, and that cry, it is style. When a man, on the contrary, *communicates* only a thought to us, without baring his breast, we do not listen, whatever he might say. The thinker, who does not know how to write, dissimulates what goes on inside him, and does not present to us but the dead effect of its operations. A greater writer lets us participate in the very conception of the works he gives us. In that transparent tree, one sees the sap circulating. Genius and childhood have one admirable trait in common: naïvety! They both possess that transparency that permits us to apperceive their thoughts at work even, to witness the interior formation of their ideas. What most resembles the man of genius in human language is the child, when he is simple.

Rhetoric has so degraded the words it uses that the ridicule produced by it threatens to affect things even. When it compliments someone on his style, it seems as though it is complimenting him on his toilette.

One must avenge speech in order to avenge ideas.

A man's style is the expression of his activity.

All creatures are placed face to face with life and face to face with themselves, face to face with others, in a certain respect.

Style is the expression of the intimate action that they exercise and which is exercised in them and on them.

All plants receive light, but each receives it in a way that is appropriate to it: they all require and expect the heat of the sun, but they receive the rays diversely. Each assimilates them in a particular fashion, by virtue of its needs, its capacities, its internal aptitudes.

The rose's style is its perfume.

Style, being the manifestation of life, opens up a broad horizon before us. No longer must we study it only on the written page; we must follow it and research it everywhere that it manifests itself, and sometimes guess it to be there where it does not show itself. Style is at first in the words; it is also in the gestures; it is also in the looks; it is in every manifestation, silence included. Silence can have a great style. Silence can be something spoken; silence can even be the pinnacle of speech, and its culminating point. In general, speech, when it is elevated and solemn, stops, because at a certain height words are lacking. It is silence that is charged then with continuing it and expressing the inexpressible. An excited silence is the supreme expression and the blossoming of speech; it is style par excellence.

What does human language understand by the following phrase: a great man?

Is he someone who has accomplished such and such a deed? No; for I defy you to define precisely the deed that is necessary to have been accomplished in order to be a great man.

Greatness is not to be found in such an act: it is in the manner in which that act is accomplished. The same act, accomplished by thousands of men, will manifest itself in a thousand different characteristics. The greatness is not in the deed, it is in the author of the deed.

Do you want a very palpable proof of that? A man is drowning. You hurry to where he disappeared; you risk your life, and you save him. But a fool and an ape who saw you, imitate you, and each of them saves a man; they will have imitated your deed, but they will not have imitated your action, they will not have taken up your style. All things being equal, imitation, even if the most habile, will always resemble more or less what I have just said. Style will always be missing. One can rob a man of everything, except his style. Style is inviolable, like the person it is the expression of.

Greatness is not determined by any exterior deed. It emerges from the sacred source.

Would its characteristic be perseverance alone? Come on! Buffon seemed to say so. He didn't know what he was talking about. If that were the case, greatness would have for a symbol the fly that buzzes for a long time next to the same ear.

Would that be a great love?

Not yet.

Would that be a great intelligence?

No, not yet; at least, not on its own. You can understand the loftiest ideas, but not express them in a great way. Your speech will betray the inferiority of your race.

I have just spoken, in spite of myself, the word speech: it is greatness's secret that was on my lips, and that escapes me.

Speech is the explosion of a person's innermost nature.

The lion does not need it in order to show his strength, to make a great effort; it betrays itself in the least of its movements. Hercules is almost always depicted at rest. One would say that his terrifying arms have nothing to do at the moment.

Lots of men have tamed horses; but nobody, looking at the tamer, who can be one of the most vulgar of men, nobody, looking at the tamer, has cried out: Behold the master of the world!

Nobody? I am mistaken: it does not happen ordinarily; but it has happened once. And yet it was a father speaking about his son. What father has ever said: "My son will be the master of the world. The sphere that I have lived in is too small for him. Let him break out and break it, given he is up to the task of breaking it."

If Philip spoke like that is it because Alexander had tamed Bucephalus, by masking the shadow of that horse which was frightening it?

Certainly not; it is because Alexander, while taming Bucephalus, had accomplished that insignificant action in an extraordinary fashion. By his manner of taming Bucephalus, he had revealed himself, and revealed himself to be master of the world.

Between Alexander taming Bucephalus and a tamer of horses practicing his profession, where is the difference?

The difference is in style.

The tamer of horses has a right to a salary.

But when Philip said to his son: "Go, take the world, Macedonia is no longer sufficient for you": that day then, Alexander, masking that fiery horse's view of its shadow, which frightened it, turning its head towards the light, employing the sun to tame it, that day then Alexander made his speech be understood and manifested himself.

It was clear for the spectators, and for Philip

himself, that Alexander had just entered into possession of his sovereignty, that Alexander had not just
conquered a horse, but himself, himself and the Orient, the Orient avid for the sun, the Orient that is
afraid of its shadow.

That is why Bucephalus has its place in history. If I was a painter, I could not depict that sovereign
too far away from Bucephalus.

Bucephalus symbolizes him in whose presence the world grows silent.

Conquest was Alexander's speech.

In the *Jardin des Plantes*, when it causes to re-
sound, by shaking them with its claws and with its
wings, the bars of its cage, as if it were breaking them
with its thought, or when it turns its head, or when it
launches into forbidden space the stare of a dethroned
sovereign, you can see the eagle's speech.

You can hear, on stormy days, the Ocean's
speech.

When Christopher Columbus cleaved with his
sword the cloud that tried to continue to mask his fatherland from him (the fatherland is the place of desire), when he obliged the light, in the name of the
eternal Verb, to reveal America to him, he gave his
speech to the world. He affirmed to it that he was the
sovereign, and when the queen of Spain appointed
him Admiral of all the Seas, he had already been so,
for a long time. His essential sovereignty had preceded his title.

The gaze of caged condors seems to hover over the deserts that they dream of, over absent deserts, over their lost possessions, and follows still the armies that they love to follow when they are free.

Sometimes sanctity shines on genius, like the sun on the Ocean. Thus said Paul. Making himself everything to everybody, with joy as well as tears, speaking words of wisdom to perfect men, desiring to be an anathema to others, he who bore the solicitude of all Churches, a prey to combats from without and terrors within, accomplishing what the Passion of Christ was missing, he showed himself to be a sovereign by bearing the weight of the empire.

Up to now, the human spirit has very often believed that to realize beauty one must disguise himself, and the disguise that one puts on is called Art. Art has been the game he played, when he wanted to parade before himself, following certain conventions.

A man of genius must stand up, speak, be listened to, and say:

From now on, I want Art to be sincere.

I want Art to stop being man's disguise, in order to become his expression.

I want Art to be the simple, naïve, and sublime explosion of splendors of the intelligence. So that Art might be beautiful, and beauty true, I want Art from now on to speak things as they are.

God will want, if I'm not mistaken, that that voice should be heard.

Ancient rhetoric has said: You are ugly, disguise yourself, for if you should show yourself such as you are, you will cause horror. Art is a disguisement; choose then a type of convention, look around you and seek: you will have merely a difficulty of choice. Imitate, feign, play a game that is pleasing to the public: beauty is a fiction. The laws of life are ugly: to please, Art must make rules for itself, independent of real laws.

Now, it is necessary that he who must found the Art of the future should purify the air sullied by these words and say:

Ugliness has, in fact, its place in man; for man is fallen. But regeneration is possible. Behold the waters of baptism.

Beauty is still permitted, – there it is, coming towards us. Grab it, dress it, and then we can present it to ourselves.

Dress it, not as a disguise, but as a splendor more real than ourselves, that we must possess and never lose. We are soiled! eh, well! let's purify ourselves. Ancient man did not dare show himself; would that the new man might be born and appear, that he might resplend in the eyes of men, not like a hero in the theater, but like a living truth, more alive than the old man he replaced. Let him appear, and let him act, that he might act in the splendor of his regenerated nature, that he might make the type gleam that he conceals, that he might release the ideal that he carries! that he might be truth! Beauty will jump up; beauty, instead of being a fiction, is the splendor of the truth. Would that Art, which was the old man's disguise, might recount in the sincerity of the phrase the splendor of the new man!

Man, absolutely unable to do without Beauty, can make efforts towards it, and can do so in two ways. He can attempt to lie to himself in the name of beauty, or to speak honestly to himself in the name of beauty. If he wants to lie to himself, he will attempt to embellish his fall and to make himself graceful in sin. If he wishes to speak honestly, he will attempt to adorn himself internally and externally with the real splendor that he is made for. Art absolutely cannot avoid beauty, it must counterfeit it by a game or possess it with effort. It must either parody it or conquer it. Art cannot not feel the natural ugliness of the old man.

It must dissimulate it, or it must strike it by lightning.

In a word, it must disguise the man who looks down, or accept, affirm, proclaim the man who looks up.

Art that is attached to the old man is obliged to apply makeup to him whom it insists on painting, for the old man is ugly, and Art, such as it is, cannot renounce beauty. Art, thus conceived, is a lie.

Art that is attached to the regenerated man can depict freely and frankly, in the candor of his genius, him whom it consents to paint, for the regenerated man is a magnificent being, and Art, by expressing him, encounters his magnificence, without sacrificing any sincerity.

Very often great artists have had for particular character, for art, for *style*, the effort that consists in embellishing fallen man with a beauty that does not belong to him, by a hidden and deceptive beauty, a beauty that exists elsewhere and that having been placed there, like an aureole over the face of evil, was a lie and a theft.

During that time, other artists, inferior artists, those who copy, not daring bravely to wrest beauty from the good so as to decorate the bad, invented by so doing a beauty of convention, which belongs neither to the good nor the bad, for it does not exist, but which is simply a form of habit. That is a disguisement, an arrangement, a convention, a habitude, a mode by virtue of which one must assume certain attitudes, while avoiding certain others, pronouncing certain words, while avoiding certain others, pronouncing them with a certain tone, and not with a certain other tone. It is in that spirit that a large quantity of tragedies are conceived. In that state of abasement, Art aspires it seems, not to beauty, but to decorum, which is the parody of beauty; it takes for law, not life, but habitude; it takes for goal, not truth, but convention. The ideal of classical tragedy ends by becoming the pattern of fashions.

It is time that Art proclaim beauty, that it draw it from where it is and say where it draws it from; in that way it is bold and simple, true and powerful; that God might give us a great artist whose style has for character the vivid splendor of sincerity!

That would be an important and magnificent study to read history from the point of view of style, that is to say, to ask of each great man the reason, the nature, of his greatness, which is his own character and the virtue of his style.

Alexander would tell us that his style is the very genius of conquest, that his way of approaching things is to dominate them; such was that man's style that the name of his horse, pronounced by him, had to receive from his lips a consecration that elevated it to the dignity of a symbol.

Caesar would tell us that his style is indicated by the words that he spoke, during the storm, to the trembling pilot: "*What are you afraid of? You are carrying Caesar.*" His expression, it is the affirmation of the empire of the world that was waiting for him. His expression, it is the tears he shed, at thirty years old, in memory of Alexander, who was already a conqueror at that age.

Homer's style, it is the first words of Priam's prayers:

"Remember your father, god-like Achilles, your father, feeble and old, just like I am..."

Those words capture Homer in his entirety, the gods, paternity, old age, strength, weakness, and the Homeric epithet itself: "god-like Achilles..."

Here is Bossuet's style: "*Madame dies, Madame is dead!*" The social grandeurs, with death close by.

Christopher Columbus' style, it is the sign of the cross traced in the fog by the tip of his sword.

It seems to me that at the solemn epoch wherein we find ourselves a great man is needed, or rather great men who speak in the name of humanity, who speak the human style and who engrave in it their different characters, their different signatures.

It seems to me that prayer is the human style par excellence; I mean to say man's expression.

What does it mean to express man? it is to tell his misery and to tell his grandeur.

Now, prayer affirms misery, it puts man on his knees, like the beggar in the Gospel! It affirms him as blind and poor, needful and supplicating.

But it affirms his grandeur in a super-eminent fashion, it shows him to us acting on God's decrees.

Through it, God introduces us into the mystery of his government, and the instant he introduces us thus into his counsels is the instant when he throws us down, face to the ground; prayer is at one and the same time a cry of distress and a hymn of glory. Now, the cry of distress and the hymn of glory are they not man's expression, are they not man's style? Man's style, it is the response of a man to the words that Moses heard:

"I am He who am."

O you who are, listen then, listen and grant!

Passions, Characters, Souls

Man has always studied man. He looks on himself with a curiosity mixed with disquietude. He admires himself, he despises himself, he surprises himself, he looks deeply into himself, he regards himself in all senses, as if he wanted to find and say, about that bizarre individual that he is, a last word, a word that has not yet been spoken. Now, to say it, that word, man must stop looking on man; but he must not stop looking at man. For to see himself, he must dominate himself. He must place himself above himself in order to know himself. He must depart from on high in order to get to the bottom. His gaze does not plunge into abysses except when it falls from mountain tops.

Art, in its studies on man, has taken a thousand forms, a thousand aspects, a thousand usages, a thousand sentiments. It has laughed, it has wept, it has shivered. It has divided itself (for man classifies all things), it has divided itself, and when true division, organic division, escaped him, he invented, by considering himself under different costumes, the mechanical division of genres. He has made tragedies, he has made comedies. In summary, what has he done?

We are going to try and sound, and measure, the depth of his different attempts.

Art can consider man in his relationship with such and such a person or thing in particular.

It can consider him in his relationships with people or things in general.

It can consider him in his relationships with himself and with infinity.

Drama and tales are born of the need that man experiences, in order to put himself on stage and look at himself. There he is, his own confidant, he sees the springs that make him act, he sees the love and hatred of beings played out before him.

But as man obeys in everything the temptation to separate himself, he often looks at a single point in himself in relation to a single object. When he looks fixedly on a single point in his interior world, and a single point in the exterior world, he arrives at the depiction of a *passion*. But life, demanding, so as to manifest itself, a complete system of feelings and actions; life demanding, so as to develop, a certain range of relations; passion, as soon as it is isolated, becomes abstract.

Falling into that trap, drama is called tragedy.

Tragedy has mistaken convention for the real and abstraction for the ideal.

The fall of the real and that of the ideal drag man in its wake.

Man, isolated from multiple elements in his life, and reduced to an isolated passion, disappears in order to make way for the *hero*.

The hero is a conventional individual who debates with himself, without living, in an abstract place.

Man is in a relationship with God. But the hero's only relationship is with fate.

The ideal replaced by the abstract: the real replaced by the conventional.

God replaced by destiny, man by the hero, nature by a vestibule.

Such are the consequences of the modern tragic system.

In life's order of things, man can isolate himself only if he isolates himself in God; there, moreover, he finds everything. God is the only confidant that suffices.

The system of comedy, because it has dispensed with nobility, excludes less things. It still excludes God, as we are going to see, and by consequence the soul: but as it does not exclude life's details completely, man can appear with his external relations, that is to say with his character.

Man's character, it is instability and weakness in life.

The hero's character, it is fixedness and aplomb in death.

Man's nature, what determines his way of being, what distinguishes him from another suchlike man, does not exist in the hero. Also, style is divers among men and common between heroes, for style is the expression of our individual speech. The style of classical tragedy is official and impersonal. It fears to name the matter, because it does not believe it to be noble, and because the isolated passion of the hero supposes only the existence of an isolated heroine and does not suppose the existence of the matter. It fears to name God for a bunch of reasons, for this reason among others that the isolated passion of the abstract hero is not attached in any way to the infinite.

In man, passion, even when it is in keeping with and, by consequence, in battle with other elements, elements of life or elements of death, is intermittent, or at least remittent: it triumphs, combats, or succumbs. In all cases, it is merely an accident of human life; the foundation that supports it is the living man; his life is distinct from his passion, can be conceived outside of his passion, has preceded it, and can survive him.

In the tragic hero, passion, even when it is isolated, and not an accident, is its very substance. The hero not existing, his passion is not supported by anything; also, the hero is not, unlike man, susceptible to changing or lying to himself. Man can be accidentally in love (I take that word in the sense that the theaters take it); man can be accidentally a traitor. Britannicus, on the contrary, not being an amorous man, but a Lover by profession, *a young first* (to continue speaking in the language of the theater, which mocks itself), Britannicus does nothing but love. He will love fatally, necessarily; and his love, because it will be isolated, will be abstract. Narcissus, not being a man who betrays, but a *traitor*, will do nothing else but betray. He will betray forever, fatally, inevitably, from the first word of his role to the last. Therefore his betrayal, in order to be continual and necessary, will be abstract. Our very indignation will vanish before the necessities of his position. He has duties to fulfill with respect to the buskin that he wears. As he is the traitor, what would he do in that vestibule, abstract like himself, if he ceased for a moment to betray? If he hands over Britannicus' secrets to Nero, he hands over also his own to the public with an extreme facility. A real traitor deceives others only because he deceives himself: he who would admit his role would become incapable of continuing. Narcissus, on the other hand, confides his plan to us.

> *And to make ourselves happy, we must rid ourselves of the poor.*

If he were complicated, that is to say human, he would be deluded; he would have, at the heart of his black deed, another feeling behind which he would hide it. But he shows it to us, that black deed, because he has nothing else to show us, and he confides his plan to us because he has only *one* plan.

He will *always* give bad counsel. On the other hand, Burrhus will always give good ones: and that compensation, far from compensating anything, will put into relief the absence of life that is shared between those two.

Orestes *loves* Hermione. (I persist in believing that that word love is employed there with irony.) Interest in his situation would be complete here: he is a miserable man, cursed by the gods, by men; he seeks refuge against his destiny in the love of an exceptional creature who would open an asylum for him against universal proscription.

That point of view is not even suggested in the tragedy. In order to expose that horizon, Orestes and Hermione would have had to be shown in the universality of their relationship: a complete Orestes would have been necessary, a complete Hermione, two living beings; it would have been necessary to show by what secret sympathy Orestes had been attracted to Hermione, a sympathy drawn from the bottom of his soul; it would have been necessary to establish a contrast, apparent at least, between Hermione and the other women, which rendered Orestes' delusion plausible, and would have explained his hope of a refuge. He would have needed to be surrounded by despair, he would have apperceived hope represented in Hermione alone: that figure would have needed to be detached, in his eyes, from the rest of the world in order to offer him some peace. Thus, his last deception would be truly terrible. The memories of childhood that could have reattached him to Hermione, if they still lingered in him, would have been heartrending; but it would have needed at first, it would have needed as a first condition that all aspects of his life were illuminated; it would have needed, with light in hand, the walking around together of Orestes and Hermione. We do not know Orestes; as for Hermione, we know merely one thing, which is that she loves Pyrrhus, or rather, for I grow tired of profaning words, that she is attracted to him, but that quality is not sufficient to interest us.

When a man loves, or is amorous even, his

love or his passion are attached to something; it has its roots somewhere; it explains itself well or poorly, but always in a certain fashion; it has been subjected to one influence or another, etc. But in order for that passion to be thus illuminated, it must be in context.

The hero is amorous by right: he is amorous, because he wears the proper costume, the lover's habit. His passion has neither a beginning nor a continuation. It is a parody of eternity.

What characterizes man, it is putting himself in relation to all things.

The hero has put a confidant between the world and himself. He has a unique and necessary outlet. He has need of that confidant who can explain his situation to the public. For personally, the hero has no need of anything.

A passion is merely one of the faces of a man's character. Comedy allows for presenting, at one and the same time, many passions, many aspects of the same individual, many exterior relationships, in a word, the characters.

From that curious point of view, Alceste is the Orestes of comedy; Mithridates is the Harpagon of tragedy.

Give Orestes permission to extend his rapports a little with the external world, do not bind him anymore to Hermione and the Furies: you have Alceste. Célimène[4] is a Hermione living, at the very least, the

---

[4]Alceste... Célimène: two characters, one male, the second female, in Molière's *Le Misanthrope*.

life of the salons. Orestes' passion for Hermione cannot be explained, because that passion has no atmosphere about it. The drama is played out in the void. Alceste's passion for Célimène can be conceived of because those two individuals not being isolated on earth, Alceste having seen other women, Eliante being there, that passion is a preference and that preference is explained by its very absurdity. The passion has a logic all its own, which is absolute absurdity.

Célimène being the woman least suitable in the world for Alceste, it is natural not that Alceste should love her, but that Alceste should be madly in love with her. (If ever troubled common sense resumes its form and its calm, I hope that Speech, having become the mirror of Thought again, will no longer call by the same name the man who loves and the man who is amorous.)

Alceste's false hatred for humanity explains the false love he conceives for Célimène. He throws himself against a reef, mistaking it for a place of safe harbor, and nothing is more natural. Seduced by the same errors that he detests, he excludes from his anger the woman who deserves it the most, and puts into evidence, by the fervor of his delusion, the truth that he fails to recognize. Take away Célimène's nature; give her, on the order of evil, other proportions; call Hermione that vivacious woman, and put her in front of Orestes, Orestes' error will be explainable: he will have to do with an actual Fury who will exempt him from pursuit by the Furies of the theater; there will be at least a reason for him losing his head, a reason for killing, a reason for dying.

Mithridates is in love! I do not insist on the ridiculousness of his position; but I ask the permission to express in a word an observation that strikes me: his love is abstract. Harpagon is in love, much like Mithridates. But in addition he is greedy. Now, his greed prevents his love from being abstract, because that greed is a second passion, which accompanies the first, which fights against it; because that greed presents to us a new side of Harpagon, and because the man who has two sides has a human character; he who has merely one side is a hero. Remove Harpagon's greed; reduce him to his isolated love; take away the contradiction that makes him a man: you have Mithridates. Molière's talent is to combine in one individual two passions that are discordant, and to place that individual in a situation that obliges him to make a choice. Tartuffe's is between his self-interest and his love; Alceste's is between his bad mood and his love; Harpagon's is between his greed and his love, etc., etc. Molière's individual is always vanquished by himself; he betrays himself at the last moment, and he excites in us the strange, but real, pleasure that we take in seeing human nature confounded.

Tragedy presents passions to us; comedy, characters; but the soul, does it appear in Molière? Never. Why not?

It is because the soul appears only when man, having come back from a serious visit to his inner core, finds there, with his passions, the memory of his destiny. That solemn re-entry into the domain of durable things so that the profundities of the human soul might be illuminated; the passions are like an anvil on the surface of the Ocean; but one must hold in hand a light unknown to the tragedies and comedies in order to plunge deeper into man and to see clearly into his abysses.

There are only supreme things that touch the soul's root. So long as its origin and its final end are totally absent from his memory, so long as those ideas do not appear either victorious, or vanquished, we have not seen the man; we have been able to see a character, for if isolated passion is the abstract man, character is the external man. Tragedy had removed from man all his relations, even external, except *one,* which was called passion. Comedy gave back to man his external relations. It restored his character to him, but it passed by, without seeing it, his soul: its gaze did not go so far.

The person who stands up while exhibiting bravado, that there is the person of tragedy; the person who bumps up against other people and things in this world, that there is the person of comedy.

The man who, in the evening, meditates willfully or by force because he is for one instant faced with himself, now that is man.

Is Molière a dramatist? No. Drama is action. What is, in this world, for us, the condition for action, for the act? It is struggle, the struggle of nature and of freedom. The human person tends toward his goal through a barred roadway; the obstacles that nature, in the widest sense of that word, opposes to his freedom, now that is the subject of drama, the principle of contradiction. Comedy has merely opposed one passion to another passion; Art, in its elevated form, would oppose passion to an idea. The triumph of human freedom over the enemy within, that is the denouement, that is the victory. Tragedies and comedies have forgotten the unique law of Art, which is the law of victory. Victory is a bought harmony.

What do we require of Art? We require deliverance. It elevates us above our present condition. It admits us into the contemplation of our ideal form. It inspires in us respect for our soul, desire, the hope to realize glimpsed splendors. The joy that it brings us is the joy of triumph: the solidarity grips our heart, and all human glories are our own. Molière refuses us those transports, because his horizon stops at our misery. Incurable weakness summons despair. The dramatic element, it is beaten weakness, transfigured by force, brought back to it, blended into it. Man will never be content if you do not speak to him about his greatness. Now, the fight, with Molière, it is not the fight of the strong or the weak, it is the fight of two weaknesses between themselves. This, instead of lifting the soul up, discourages it, by the ignominy of the choices offered. Molière is an observer, an analyst; let's not try to make a moralist out of him! He's a man of talent; let's not try to make a man of genius out of him.

Every comedy resolves in a marriage, and Molière's comedy has the effect of debasing marriage. Marriage appears in it like a convenient formality in the fifth act. It is despoiled of its divine majesty, despoiled of its human majesty. I do not think that

Molière's cramped head contained, even for one instant, a single idea of the sacrament. Marriage is for
him the result of a passion and an intrigue, then the
means to make the curtain fall. Now, passion and intrigue are things too inferior to be associated with the
idea of marriage. Harmony, under all its facets, having escaped Molière, marriage must have escaped him
as well, inevitably. His horrible love is one of the
most hideous forms of hatred, an anticipation of eternal hell.

Love, in comedy, when it is not the complicity
of a rogue and a rascal, is the cold delusion of two id-
iots. God is forgotten, man is degraded, heaven is
closed for entry, the earth is frozen over; one grows
bored, one is mistaken, the curtain falls, and all is said
and done.

Whence comes it that Molière is hopeless in
his denouements? (I believe La Harpe agrees with
me, but I do not have the courage to verify it; life is
too short to re-read La Harpe.)

Molière is hopeless in his denouements, because he has never given God his due. He has ignored
the very essence of denouement, that is to say the in-
vasion of a thought hovering over the events, gather-
ing them to it, illuminating them, pacifying them,
transfiguring them.

Molière spent his entire life looking at isolated
weaknesses whose cause he did not inquire into; never has he said: "This man that I observe is a fallen being." He sees this or that fall; but he does not see the
fall in and of itself; he studies, one after the other, the

partial manifestations of it; he does not penetrate them, he does not shed a light on them. Also, if he has known some human characters, he has never measured man. He has not suspected either our loftiness or our abysses; he has ignored all our glories. Neither memories, nor regrets, nor aspirations, nor enthusiasms have an echo in his work. The wind from the mountains has not blown on him: the origin of man has not disquieted him; he has not recognized our titles to nobility; he exposes our wounds and declares them incurable. His work is the opposite of a work of art. Art delivers, Molière enslaves.

How to resolve in a superior harmony the contradictions that stir us, that glorious vocation of Art, Molière hasn't got the faintest idea. He does not even take the trouble to deny the light: he ignores that it exists. In place of a celestial smile, it is a mocking smile that he leaves us with for adieu. The curtain falls, and we have not seen the rainbow. Hope, which Schlegel has called the very character and distinctive sign of the human species on earth, hope has not said a word.

Nor do you hear in Molière the expression of repentance. Repentance is the sign of great souls. Innocence even recognizes it, I do not know by what sympathetic reflection: a marvelous solidarity, unifying it with the guilty, allows it to shed tears that, without repentance, it would be deprived of.

The tragic system, as I said at the beginning of this study, has not considered man except from the point of view of a unique, isolated, abstract passion: comedy, in the place of men, has depicted characters.

The soul has not been touched.

It is important to distinguish with effort ancient art from modern art, ancient tragedy from modern tragedy.

Modern tragedy has replaced God with fate, and man with the hero; but neither fate, nor the hero, are two living beings, they are two handy abstractions for a man who writes in Alexandrine verse.

In ancient tragedy, God is replaced by destiny: but that destiny is not abstract; it has, in the mind of the author, a frightening personality. Also, the error that floats above its work, it is a serious error, instead of an error of complaisance.

It is fate that pursues the modern Orestes.

It was destiny that pursued the ancient Orestes.

In modern tragedy, fate is ridiculous.

In ancient tragedy, destiny was terrible.

In modern tragedy, we regret the absence of man, because the hero, who replaces him, does not satisfy us completely.

In ancient tragedy, man has, up to a certain point, the right not to appear totally complete, because he is not the subject of the drama: he is the actor in it, he is the victim. Men of ancient tragedy are moved by the strings that destiny holds in its hands, and the true drama happens on Olympus.

The individuals still represent passions, but they are no longer the passions of man, they are the passions of destiny.

We are, as we often say in France, the most spiritual people and the most derisive of the rest of the world, but nevertheless we continue to shudder for over two hundred years now, with an imperturbable seriousness, when listening, in the Théâtre-Français, to *Orestes Pursued by the Furies*.

I have seen *Andromache* several times on the stage: I looked into the face of the actor condemned to pronounce these lines:

> *But what do I see? In my eyes Hermione embraces him;*
> *She wants to save him from the blow that menaces him.*
> *Gods! what dreadful looks she gives me!*
> *What demons, what serpents does she drag behind her?*
> *Hey there! daughters of hell, are your hands ready?*
> *The serpents hissing on your head – who are they for?*
> *Whom do you target with the engine that follows you?*

One asks oneself, in spite of oneself, in spite of the lessons of experience, if the actor, gripped by a most legitimate and real fury such as Orestes was gripped by, will not stop short before that tirade, overcome by the energetic feeling that is the consciousness of ridiculousness. In Greek tragedy, the Eumenides live and breathe; they are the main characters. Orestes is only there because they need a victim, but they do not leave him! The air, around him, is evidently poisoned. Whether one sees them or does not see them, one thinks of them, one waits for them.

Orestes does not need, in order to hold our interest, to be a complete man; he is given to us merely as a victim, and it is in that way that we accept him.

The piece takes place in hell.

Fatality weighs on Orestes from the moment he speaks his first words, and, when it reveals itself, nobody has the right to be surprised.

But in Racine's tragedy, the Furies have no role whatsoever. Orestes is a lover and an ambassador; he pays compliments to Pyrrhus, and he makes declarations to Hermione. Fatality is absent. Orestes did not kill his mother, or, if he killed her, he no longer remembers. The Furies have forgotten him for five acts, and when they arrive, there is no more time. After a love affair, he declares to us in elegant lines of verse that he will see them again. That unexpected communication, which the guards of his retinue oppose with complete indifference, surprises us, without frightening us. The girls of hell, together with the machinery that follows them, instead of coming, as Orestes thinks, to take him away into eternal night, appear with the so very un-infernal intention of delivering a tirade that prepares us for the curtainfall.

Greek tragedy is more serious. It manifests Fatality under different forms and under different passions. For Greek Fatality has passion.

Œdipus is another Orestes. Accused of madness by his children, Sophocles, to justify himself, displayed the spectacle of incurable Fatality before his judges. He was, at that solemn instant, the representative of Greek art; in all countries, the accusation of madness would have been dropped, but in Greece it had to be taken as the election of wisdom itself and its beloved expression.

But in order to penetrate Greek tragedy, one must seize it at its source, in Homer. Greek tragedy is a comment on the *Iliad*:

> *Μνῆσαι πατρὸς σοῖο θεοῖς ἐπιείκελ' Ἀχιλλεῦ,*
> *Be mindful of your father, etc.*

That is the culminating point of Homer's genius.

But what is the meaning of that supreme prayer? What does King Priam represent, Priam the old, Priam the father of Hector, kneeling before Achilles? What is the meaning of the *Iliad*? Is the *Iliad* a tale of the siege of Troy?

Let's go!

The *Iliad* is the tableau of Achilles' anger, and the poet declares as much to us in the first line of verse:

> *μῆνιν ἄειδε θεὰ Πηληϊάδεω Ἀχιλῆος, etc. etc.*
> *Muse, sing the anger, etc., etc.*

The literary education of the French, a very superficial education, to employ the gentlest term for it, is rather often limited to their own works, and by the same stroke it removes any chance of intelligence, for to know France in a vacuum is to be profoundly ignorant of it.

Proof of the actual personality of the man who was Homer is found, I believe, in the subject of the *Iliad* thus considered. If the poem treated of the Trojan War, it could be, as one has thought, the work of many authors: the cyclical poets have spoken in a similar way as Homer: they have treated of the same subjects; they have taken everything from their master, even his old Ionian dialect. Arctinus de Milet has recounted the Trojan War from the death of Hector to the battle between Ajax and Ulysses. Leschès de Lesbos has continued his work and followed the events leading up to the taking of Troy; Augias de Trézène, in his poem νοστοι has told of the return of the Greek chiefs: but none of them have combined and grouped the facts around that terrible moral unit: Achilles' anger. Homer, by declaring in the first lines of the *Iliad* that he makes the inaction of Achilles the action of his poem, leaves us, with the mark of his genius, the proof of his personality and his actual existence.

Genius is not collective.

Now, here, I believe, is how one must understand the *Iliad* in order to follow its history through Greek literature, which is the development of it.

Achilles is Destiny; Hector, Humanity.

Achilles, in his hatred, punishes in a characteristic fashion; he does not punish by striking, he punishes by withdrawing; he says to Agamemnon:

"Go, shepherd of peoples and king of kings: I leave you to your powerfulness; you are the master, do what you can while I am not there. I am retiring to my tent."

Achilles' tent is the temple of superior divinity among the Greeks. It is the sanctuary of Destiny. Achilles is Destiny.

Hector is man; Hector's family is Humanity. The human family appears, in Homer, represented by Andromache; in one smile by her, Homer has brought together all the joys and tears: $\delta\alpha\chi\rho\upsilon\omicron\epsilon\nu\ \gamma\epsilon\lambda\alpha\sigma\alpha\sigma\alpha$.

But Destiny leaves its immobility to crush man: Achilles kills Hector.

And Priam is on his knees before him who has his hands tainted with the blood of his son.

Humanity demands mercy of vanquishing Destiny.

In Greek tragedy, it is Destiny that continues the role of Achilles; it is Humanity that continues the role of Hector; it is the chorus that, dispatching its counsels to earth and its prayers to heaven, continues the role of Priam. Greek tragedy converges on Priam's prayer as if toward its summit or rather its center, and falls short of it.

In the *Iliad*, power, the divine element, belongs to the Greeks. Humanity and weakness are on the side of Troy. Ancient Rome wanted to invert the situation: it put the gods in the hands of Aeneas. But Virgil was actually incapable of imitating Homer; he wrote a parody.

Homer does not dominate just cyclical poetry, Greek tragedy, and Latin poetry (if this last one is allowed); he dominates Greek prose; he is the teacher of Herodotus. Herodotus recounts history in the same style as Homer. He is brilliant like him, naïve and superficial like him in certain terms.

He mixed in everything: Destiny, gods, men, peoples.

Aeschylus represented Destiny in battle with Humanity itself. Prometheus is his typical conception. Aeschylus does not paint this or that passion. He describes in broad strokes an immense battle that he does not understand well. He sees only from afar and through a cloud the subject of drama that he writes about. He has heard say that man attempted something against Divinity, and what did he attempt? He has no idea. He thinks that man was punished. Will he always be? He knows nothing about it, but he thinks so, because his divinity is Fatality, the sovereign and sovereignly inexorable goddess.

Aeschylus heard the distant echo of disfigured traditions. Aeschylus looks into neither the tragedy of individuals nor the tragedy of peoples; he contemplates the tragedy of Humanity. He is more elevated than Homer and less accessible than him. More epic than tragic, he employs theater but only by chance. The drama of the Eumenides is entitled: *The Eumenides*. Aeschylus does not hide his thinking from us. He names his principal character first; he does not ask forgiveness for having put him on stage.

Aeschylus leads Destiny onto the scene in order to crush Humanity before it; Sophocles presents Destiny to us as well, but with him it is no longer in battle with humankind, as represented by tradition; it is in battle with various peoples. The epic becomes tragedy, the tragedy becomes national; instead of Prometheus and the Eumenides, instead of cold, universal terror, we have Ajax, Electra, Œdipus, Antigone, Philoctetes, we have the Greeks. Œdipus is an Orestes nationalized in Greece, circumscribed in a point in space. Sophocles puts into play the passions of Destiny in battle against peoples.

Euripides will attain the passion of individuals: Andromache, Iphigenia, Hippolyta are going to appear; they will not appear, as in Aeschylus, in order to represent humankind; they will not appear, as in Sophocles, to represent Greece: they will appear in Euripides as man; only, those men will be the playthings of the power that devours Prometheus and that pursues Œdipus; that same Destiny, implacable, deaf and dumb, that devours humankind, on the terrible rock, in the person of Prometheus, that pursues Greek sovereignty in the person of Œdipus, hounds individuals nows; it is Phaedra whom Euripides will deliver to the vulture, like Aeschylus delivered Prometheus to it; but Prometheus is Humanity, and Phaedra is a woman; she is an individual.

In the Greek tragedy *Hippolytus*, the principal personage, it is Aphrodite.

His extreme inferiority with respect to his two predecessors could be explained by this one consideration alone: Aeschylus and Sophocles appealed to Greek thought. Aeschylus appealed to the needs of ancient Greece which lent an ear to vague murmurs, Oriental murmurs; Sophocles responded to the needs of a more modern Greece, to that Greece that was forgetting Asia, that was losing its memory of Troy, that was becoming more insular, that was concentrating all its forces in itself, in order to found its nationality, and to glorify itself for being Greece. That contracted Greece summoned Sophocles, and Sophocles came. But Greece has never been occupied by individuals. Also Euripides, who would have liked to depict the individual, had his hands tied by the system of Fatality. The fatalistic doctrine is as entirely false with his predecessors as it is with him: but, next to their errors, outside of them, his predecessors had found a place, in their large conceptions, for beauty and ample developments; that amplitude, which furnished Aeschylus with its subjects and its nature, was lacking in Euripides: Euripides was bound to his dry and narrow error. One can say of him, as of his heroine:

> *It was nothing but Aphrodite attached to his*
> *[prow...*

Euripides dies, like Phaedra, suffocated by Destiny.

The passions of Destiny in combat with individuals are the subject of his work.

Greek comedy presents to us, like modern comedy, characters: but Aristophanes is much less human and much more local that Molière. The characters of Greek comedy are absolutely Greek characters, pure and simple: also, they have no eternal interest: posterity does not recognize them. Greek comedy is always occupied with the fatherland, never with humanity. In order to understand it, one must know what was, after the Persian wars, the pride of Athens, queen of the islands in the Aegean sea, which thought itself queen of the human spirit. If Aristophanes had had so decisive an influence on Socrates' fate, it was that he saw, in that man, not the individual who bore the name of Socrates, but the veritable representative of Athenian character, the most subtle of sophists, *the professor of irony*.

We have cast a eye on French tragedy, we have found its conventions, its passions, its heroes; we have looked at modern comedy, we have found its characters; we have interrogated ancient tragedy, it responded to us: Fatality! If we should interrogate ancient comedy, it would show us, like modern comedy, its characters, but that would be the characters of peoples, and no longer the characters of men. Will we not see its soul appear?

We cut through the fog of the North in order to ask about its secrets.

Give to Orestes, I was saying, permission to extend a little his relationship with the external world: you have Alceste.[5]

I add: put to Orestes and to Alceste the philosophical problem, without resolving it: you have Hamlet.

Orestes, Alceste, and Hamlet are the same man presented in tragedy, in comedy, in drama. Hamlet's situation and Orestes' offer an analogy that ought not to have escaped anyone. Both are charged

---

[5]Alceste: the protagonist of Molière's *The Misanthrope*.

with avenging their father assassinated by their mother; both consider it a crime to avenge him, and a
crime not to avenge him. Both are persecuted by irre-
sistible powers that give them orders that are equally
terrible to obey and to resist.

What is more, Hamlet resembles Alceste by
his disgust of men, by indecision, by the madness of
his love. But what is pleasant in Alceste is terrible in
Hamlet, because Hamlet has a soul and Alceste does
not. Alceste is nothing more than a character.

Hamlet has a soul: but that soul, will it crack?
No. It is in paralysis. What paralyzed Orestes was fatality; what paralyzes Hamlet is chance. Chance is the
modern word for fatality. Hamlet doubts: doubt is the
theoretical expression of the doctrine of chance; the
man who doubts believes in chance. Hamlet's God is
doubt, his cult is chance.

To be or not to be, that is the formula of the
prayer that is needed for that God. The sacrifice he
demands is the death given by Chance. One kills oneself without knowing why or how. Doubt triumphs
and Chance is satisfied. The god Chance asks with a
blind and indifferent fury for the death of both the
good and the bad, the innocent and the guilty; but the
guilty don't expiate, and the innocent don't redeem:
Chance strikes without a target, and man dies for no
reason. One strikes in order to strike, one kills in order to kill, one dies in order to die; one goes away because one must make way for others, and that's all
there is to it.

Hamlet is the apotheosis of doubt, its deification. Now, the triumph of doubt, it is to reign over a man that sees. Hamlet sees the ghost of his father and doubts the immortality of the soul.

M. de Châteaubriand says somewhere that Hamlet, who chats with a revenant, *ought to know what he is dealing with*.

M. de Châteaubriand did not realize that he was reproaching Shakespeare for the supreme beauty of his work. By giving to that man, who is the very incarnation of doubt, the physical view of what he doubts, without taking from him his doubt, Shakespeare has shown a stroke of genius. The very spirit of his father, showing himself to him, speaking with him, does not succeed in making him affirm anything. Pursued by an immortal soul, he doubts the immortality of the soul. To die, to sleep, to dream perhaps? And he has just spoken with his dead father!

For the man who *wants* to doubt, doubt is possible in the presence of dug up graves. Shakespeare tells us it magnificently, and M. de Châteaubriand did not get it.

Hamlet loves Ophelia; but he pushes his doubt to the point of doubting his love. As long as she lives, he pushes her away; he realizes he loves her when he sees her buried.

He has a thirst for vengeance; but, persecuted by doubt, in his last retrenchment, he hesitates before vengeance, without inclining towards forgiveness. On the point of slitting the throat of the murderer of his father, he recoils, he says, in the fear of sending him to heaven if chance should have it that he is in a state of grace. It is a pretext, a defeat.

He wants neither to punish nor to forgive. He rests immobile, pinned down by doubt, which interdicts him everything at once. He turns towards Ophelia; he doubts her; towards himself, and he doubts himself; towards heaven, and he doubts God. The ideal appears to him on the horizon, like a chariot of fire carrying away what he loves. With a fixed and avid gaze, he follows the tracks of the wheels on the burning dew, then he stops, arms crossed, incapable of acting, incapable also of renouncing. He closes his eyes, leaving to chance the care for his love and for his hatred.

Without wishing to study Shakespeare today from all points of view, I cannot help acknowledging that in *Hamlet,* as everywhere else, there is at every instant a lack of simplicity. He has been reproached for lacking taste. One must get rid of that word which is bad in itself, and which also has been degraded by critics of the lower rung, by those arrangers of words. But it is true that Shakespeare often lacks the eternal laws of that superior common sense that I would like to call the wisdom of art and which has simplicity for its character. Enemies of poetry too often affect to confound it with disorder so that we might not seize each occasion to avenge it. It bears saying and repeating that art and reason cannot be in contradiction, and that Shakespeare, each time he has sinned against common sense, has sinned against poetry, which is the splendor of common sense.

Let's pass over to the Rhine. Chance will be

replaced by the void, Hamlet by Faust; Hamlet doubts, Faust denies and scoffs. Mephistopheles has replaced the shadow of death. Hamlet had said: Being and Non-Being are uncertain; Faust said: Being and Non-Being are identical.

Hegel has passed by there: his hand dug up the abyss where art and life were buried.

Germany has had the last word on all error. One could say that by dint of exaggerating death, it prepares for its resurrection. Installed like vertigo at the foot of the precipice, it looks at the travelers, and it tempts them, it calls to them: Hegel, Goethe, Beethoven loan it their terrible voice; those who lean towards them are attracted; but the future will see pilgrims who grimp up the mountain, who attain, after they have surpassed the clouds, the domains of art and serenity; who turn their gaze towards the pole star, saved from the abyss.

Courage

There is no shortage of men who believe that Voltaire and Rousseau were bold spirits, intrepid men, courageous thinkers, who perhaps sinned by the excess of force and grandeur.

If public common sense were not clouded, if ideas were in their proper place, if elementary things were known, if men knew what thinking was, what courage was, what strength was, one would see that Voltaire and Rousseau were cowardly and mediocre flatterers of the ignoble eighteenth century.

To serve God is to rule: many men who admit that principle admit also the opposite of that principle.

Those men think that there is a certain glory, imprudent perhaps, but sublime in reality, in shaking off the yoke of truth and that, in the act of getting rid of it, one will dominate it.

They think that there is more greatness in saying no than in saying yes, even when speaking to absolute Truth.

That is one of the ruses that the self-love of Satan employs.

Satan cannot say: I have succeeded; but he tries to say: I have succumbed nobly, because I was too great to obey. Also, when he writes novels, when he creates melodramas, he emphatically crowns the crime as *heroic*, and permits granting to virtue approbation mixed with a certain disdain.

The fact is that man has a need for admiring; he is not content with merely approving, he must admire. Cold esteem is never what will lead the world; what leads the world is enthusiasm.

Do you want to know the path that that young man will take? Do not ask yourself what he esteems, ask yourself what he admires.

Eh, well! the devil has persuaded men that the more one is outside the law, the greater one is, and that obedience belongs to the weak.

If that were true, God would be the smallest of beings, for it is the Law.

To tell men a paradox and persuade them of it, nothing is easier; but to tell them what is evident, elementary, fundamental is to want to pass for a fool.

If there is something in the world that is evident and elementary, it is that infinite greatness belongs to God alone. So, finite greatness augments proportionally as a created being augments its resemblance to an uncreated being.

Now, a created being's resemblance to an uncreated being depends on the faithfulness with which the created being freely fulfills the law of the uncreated being; God eternally obeys the law that is He: to obey him is to imitate him; to obey him is to resemble him.

He who is Order, he has *ordered* everything; and how can human expression, which remains beautiful in spite of ourselves, not alert us to the things that it expresses?

To order is to put things in *order*.

To order is to give an *order*.

God's orders are the applications of Order, which is God.

Our conformity with infinite greatness, which is Order and which orders, being the measure of our finite greatness, the more man obeys, the more he grows.

But such is the dupery inflicted by Satan on many men, that M. de la Palisse, if he spoke philosophy, would seem paradoxical.

And in fact he would say that two and two make four.

"That's right," Voltaire himself would respond. (I believe he knew enough mathematics to go that far.)

"Four and four," M. de la Palisse would continue, "make eight."

VOLTAIRE

In fact.

M. DE LA PALISSE

Eight and eight make sixteen.

VOLTAIRE

Agreed.

M. DE LA PALISSE

You see: we can understand each other, by building on that principle that two and two make four; we even understand each other perfectly.

VOLTAIRE

We understand each other perfectly, my dear friend, and I am happy for it.

M. DE LA PALISSE

But, if instead of agreeing with me that two and two make four, you had told me, "two and two make five," would we have been able to travel along at the same pace while continuing down the path? Could we have said at the same time: Four times two makes eight?

VOLTAIRE

We could not; the point of departure would have been false.

M. DE LA PALISSE

Eh, well! if it were a matter of speaking about God, or man, is it not good to have, at the start, both one and the other, a correct and elementary idea? Is it better, when one disserts, to have a clear idea of the subject, or a clouded idea? To cloud the principle, before drawing consequences from it, is that courage or madness? A mathematician who would debut with these words: two and two make five, would he have a noble audacity or a temerity both foolish and imbecilic? Now, that imbecilic madness that destroys all knowledge by clouding every idea, that madness is yours. That's what I had, me, de La Palisse, to teach you. Transport the truths that we have just confirmed in the mathematical sciences into the terrain of moral sciences, and remember the lesson that M. de La Palisse has given to you.

What then is the use of courage?

It is to obey the truth.

It is to put fundamental ideas in their place.

It is to establish, in science and in art, elementary truths, which are the highest, the broadest, the most fecund, the deepest; it is to make no concession for error.

In a word, it is in favor of truth over error that courage must act.

Courage is the heart in action: the heart has to love beauty, and action has to serve it.

However those who, in the literary field, have thought themselves courageous, have cried: Ugliness is beauty.

They do not even know, those brave fellows, over which river the wind had passed that blew on them. They had neither understood nor heard the word order: but the vibrations in the air carried it to them, and they repeated it instinctively. Oh! what a pretty story one could amuse oneself by writing! It would be entitled: *Hegelian Without Knowing It.*

Innovations are sterile: memory alone is fecund.

There is nothing new, but there are young things: they are the pasture of genius, which loves eternal aliments.

Would that God might give us men of genius then, that we might hear nothing new!

Then we will hear simple things, *that we believe we are hearing for the first time*, for genius makes one feel the youthfulness of eternal things, while mediocre men believe that eternity is going to die of old age.

A man of genius is the rendezvous that God gives men, that they might come to work and rest under his shade.

But do you want to know in what way literatasters represent genius? They talk about it like a blind man talks about colors, and this is what they say!

I remember a drama wherein a character, who was represented to us as the epitome of the great artist, makes all imaginable follies, and to the observations that one is allowed to make to him, he responds pompously: "If you take away my confusion, you will take away my genius."

And so that the theory might see the light of day, the piece is entitled: *Disorder and Genius*.

If that aberration was particular to one man, I would not call it out. But it reveals the state of minds;

it tells us what people think who do not think at all. Those who speak to men give them those lessons, and men abandon themselves to the disorder in their mind, believing that they engage in genius.

Have you sometimes chatted with a man? If you have had that advantage, you must have heard this phrase: *Oh! that is quite simple.*

And, in the mind of your interlocutor, that phrase means this: Oh! that is not very fine, that is not very great, that is not very marvelous.

In the head of men who have never reflected, simplicity allies itself with mediocrity and contradicts splendor.

They do not even realize that simplicity is the first element, the essential principle of all splendor, that simplicity is absolutely incompatible with mediocrity.

Would that God might give to the world men of genius, then we will see some simple things.

The man of genius resembles a child who is really a child.

He does not at all resemble a man of talent, who is complicated.

The man of genius is a transfigured child: he has the gift of not aging. He has the gift of always being surprised in the face of things that are not simple; he has the gift of not habituating himself to this world: for to habituate himself to this world is to forget the other. Genius resembles a magnificent memory; but that memory is not something of the past, it is the memory of what does not occur.

Genius resembles also the intellectual conscience of humanity. Humanity, like man, repugns listening to his conscience; and also, like him, he submits.

Genius is a complaint. Natural truths, which humanity holds the secret to, warn with its voice.

When genius speaks, Satan tells men: "But you know what it says for a long time now; you have no need to listen."

In fact, genius, which is the internal voice of the human race, never says anything new, it never does anything but recall.

The genius is a poet, he is a creator, his name marks him; replace the Greek word with the Latin word, poet and creator are synonyms. But those who think that genius and disorder are synonyms believe that poetry and madness are synonyms too.

They do not know what poetry wants to tell creation, nor that the law of all creation is order. But ideas are so profoundly clouded in our intelligences that we have forgotten the meaning of words and that the word that means creation has signified for us deceit, that is to say destruction.

Genius assuming to the highest degree, in him who possesses it, the courage of the intellectual order, assumes it, to a certain measure, in those who accept it.

The courage of a man of genius consists in waiting for the hour when glory will make bow before him those who were unable to make him bow before them, and in resting orderly while waiting.

The courage that is asked of him is always to obey the truth: the courage he demands of others is not to obey error.

Now, the worst of errors is that which is consecrated by opinion. Rather remarkable thing! what does not kneel before God kneels before the devil. He who refuses his adhesion to the infinite word submits to the incomprehensible yoke of some imbeciles whom he despises. He who does not dare greet glory because it always demands some sacrifice from him, even to be contemplated, lies prostrate before reputation, which asks nothing more of him.

Genius is such a majesty that its least servants still have need of being great, they need courage, and I think that God keeps their recompenses, which will surprise them.

But the mediocre man, who has some reputation, does not ask of his friends anything but their cowardice: he begs them only to repeat what they heard said.

The first condition of intellectual courage is absolute good faith. There are two kinds of good faith: the first consists in not lying to others; the second in not lying to oneself.

That second form of sincerity is perhaps the most rare of virtues. Conversation, reading, the habit of repeating mechanically certain things previously heard, attaching certain proper names to certain epithets, a thousand unavowed and unnoticed influences dictate to the immense majority of men certain words they believe to pronounce in their name.

Offer them an unknown work of art: they wait for your opinion before daring to give their own. Magnificent punition! curious contradiction and which one does not notice! Mediocrity, which has so much vanity, so much confidence in itself, so much stubbornness above all, always has fear to believe and fear to tell.

It has neither the courage to speak up, nor the courage to admit that it does not speak up. It waits for victory to speak, and as it is as clumsy as it is timid, it finishes always by repenting for its having been a coward.

The man who, on reading for the first time the first page written by a child just out of secondary school, judges it as if that page were admired by all those around him since his childhood, that man is as great as the greatest of men; and if that child who consults with him becomes a man of genius, whatever he might do in the future, he will do nothing greater; he will not surpass the greatness of him who, the first, dared to proclaim his. He who, the first, says: "Walk!" to a great man, will himself walk beside that great man and will walk as his equal, in virtue of that law: to understand is to equal; and posterity, which separates so many names, will not separate their two names.

To submit to truth, to shake off error, now those are the two poles of courage.

The man who would say: "I am going to seek out the night and even, if I can, extinguish the sun, in order not to see clearly anymore," would surprise his equals.

The man who proposes the same reasoning with respect to God does not surprise his equals, because we are more familiar with the laws of matter than those of the spirit.

That man adds: "When I have made the night, I will go into a cave full of pits dug into the surface of the earth, without guard-rails, and I will walk in the darkness, in the company of toads and spiders, until I fall into one of those pits, which cannot take long. Others, one says, have done it before me; I intend to imitate their courage."

And we, we admire.

"God! how dark that cave is," the public cries out, "and how deep that pit is!"

The face of the intellectual world would change tomorrow and God should see, from the height of heaven, some great things, if writers, the thought-leaders of this poor world, knew what a cowherdess knows, in the far corners of Brittany, as she prepares for first communion. Not one of you would be accepted to stand beside her at an examination of catechism, if men, less vain, and by consequence less dupes, stopped admiring, with infernal good-naturedness, both annoying and mortal, obscure

and fatal things that serious practical jokers present to
them with a solemn attitude.

The Critic

The critic! You must have heard this word pronounced sometimes, doubtless. But he who pronounced it, did he understand its meaning? I do not think so. There are few words more misunderstood. If a literary critic existed in Paris today, the face of the world would be changed in one week.

The critic, such as he habitually practices his craft, is a cowardly and complacent chatterbox, who does not know how to speak, nor can, nor dares to. M. Paul, the critic, knows M. Pierre, the writer; he must treat him considerately, no matter what M. Pierre does. What's more, M. Pierre is admired by M. Jacques: so M. Paul is expected to admire him. What's more, M. Paul has nothing to say: he has no idea, no style, no desire, no regret, no horizon. He finds it quite simple that M. Pierre resemble him, applaud him, and there you have it. Or better still, M. Paul read in his childhood some book that was signed by an old and well-known name; since that time, M. Paul admires that book and proposes it as a model to writers of the future. M. Paul is strongly convinced that all the books he read in his childhood are sacred, but that no superior man anymore has the right to be born and that the creator is tired. Like Buffon and Bernardin de Saint-Pierre, M. Paul thinks that there is nothing left to say.

How many times, while looking at Paris, have I said to myself: My God, poor city! So many lost forces stir in its bosom! While cold mediocrity gaily

arrives at an easy success, how many misled or captive intelligences have not found, for want of a guide
or support, their path or their deliverance! How many
young men who perhaps had life in them, coldly repulsed by hostility or indifference, persecution more
terrible still, repulsed by indifference that detests attempts made against it, and condemned without re-
demption to remain themselves, despite the injunction
by pedants who want each man to resemble himself,
and that no man should rise above the known bar!
What a fine job that is, being a critic, running through
the world wrecking justice like a Hercules!

Ask yourself for a moment what would happen in Europe and in the world if the justice of Art
should rise up in Paris over the living and dead! Suppose for an instant (do not have fear, it's a dream),
suppose for an instant that that justice of intelligences
rose up today, with the sun of God, over the sleeping
city! Suppose that it was given to men to feel for a
second their heart beating in accord with the truth, to
shake off the iron hammer that paralyzes, that crushes
their shoulders, their backs, and their eyes, only to
wake up again in a vibrant light, in the face of true
beauties, emptied of the old lessons that they have repeated since childhood, filled with a youthful love for
what does not grow old; suppose that today's sun
shined on that spectacle in Paris, and guess what tomorrow's sun would shine on, over the face of the
globe.

But discouragement, that terrible ruse from
hell is there and paralyzes the soul and holds back the
arm. "You will not do everything," it says; "rather,

you will do nothing." But, in truth, is that a reason?

Must one, in order to speak, wait for everyone to be persuaded in advance, and because there are deaf people, does speech forfeit its rights?

I do not think so. Let us speak in spite of the deaf. Let us speak of the critic such as he is, and of the critic such as he ought to be.

If I say to the little critic that he is mediocre and silly, I will not surprise him much. Men take their mediocrity in stride, in the conviction where they stand that one cannot be anything else, unless one should fall into exaggeration.

But if I tell him that he is cruel, that little critic, I will surprise him for, not taking himself seriously, he does not take the wounds that his cold and gloved hand administer seriously: I tell him that as he is incapable of edifying whatever it might be, that he is capable of destroying a lot; that, without the strength to give life, he has the power to give death, by dint of being weak; and that to stop being cruel, he would need to become intelligent; at that time, not understanding what I am trying to tell him anymore, he responds that I am going a little too far. He will tell me that he does not intend to give death. "Eh! I am not talking about your intentions! I know very well that you have no intentions; but, but... here is what I reproach you with: you ought to be upset."

I insist on the cruelty of the unintelligent critic because one must rely on practical truths. One must tell the person who judges that height, breadth, and depth are not objects of luxury for him, but laws.

Offer an unknown work of art to a vulgar critic; he will wait for your opinion before daring to ven-
ture his. Before forming an opinion, he will consult
all his interests and the faces of all his friends. Having
exhausted his kindness on the ancients, he has nothing but stiffness and indifference for those who fight,
who suffer, who have need of some courage.

Change the signature of a work, the pages that
he found crazy earlier appear sublime to him, and
vice versa.

He flatters, he annoys, he persecutes.

In general, the little critic believes that everything is impossible, he does not admit as *being possible* anything but what he is used to. Now, he is not
used to genius, as he treats it as he treated, several
years ago, locomotives and electric telegraphs. As for
the genius of men already dead, he proclaims it with
abandon, without knowing what he says, because he
is in the habit of proclaiming, and besides he scarcely
believes in the existence of those fellows. He uses
both hands to hurl abstract silver crowns at abstract
people, which cost him nothing to distribute, for they
do not exist. That the past should have its glories, he
consents to that, for he believes neither in the past nor
in glory; but the present? but the future? let's go!

Also, that polite, correct, syrupy, and mediocre critic has nothing but conventional opinions, pru-
dent admirations, official enthusiasms. He will not
absolve you for being modern, unless you are at the

same time mediocre; he has, for mediocrity, I do not
know what tender condescension, he recognizes himself and takes pleasure in it. Then too, when he consents not to find it irreproachable, he always forgives
it; he overlooks everything. The mediocre man is the
adored child, he is the Benjamin of narrow-minded
criticism. He has weaknesses for it. It suffices that
mediocrity be mediocrity to have access to the indulgence of that critic. For the defects of mediocrity are
mediocre themselves, and thereby sympathetic to the
critic I speak of: they are erased, and all that is erased
pleases him. The superior man's defects attest to a
lively personality that unfolds, and the little critic detests them, not because they are defects, but because
they are energetic. Soft and dead, he loves what is
soft and dead. Fearing that the man armed with an
idea does not let out a cry that one is not in the habit
of hearing, he prefers, and a lot, those who write but
say nothing: those there are more submissive to him:
he is pleased with them and recognizes himself in
them. He forbids a man to be himself and orders him
to resemble someone else; he calls that being severe.
Before admiring, he searches through his habits to see
if he ordinarily admires what is before his eyes, or
analog things, and, in the name of good taste, he refuses passage to all beauty whose details he does not
know in advance. He does not judge to judge, he
judges to please his own judges; also, he loves those
who repeat stock phrases, because they do not com-
promise; he knows that that money has currency;
stock phrases are old acquaintances who do not
frighten him; but the man who speaks his own language is a young man for his contemporaries, before

being a great man for posterity. The little critic, persuaded that great men have never been young, not even alive, that for all time they were ancient, for four thousand years dead, sniggers and turns away when faced with a present and living greatness. The horror that he has for genius is mixed with shame. Before that stranger, he blushes to be himself. Before genius, greatness would consist in effacing oneself; but the little critic never effaces himself, he holds himself straight and upright. To avenge himself, he points out, in the creations of genius, the comma that is missing, and mediocrity applauds.

Whatever reason one might wish to attribute to that strange fact, mediocrity is never disconcerted. It wants this world to be its prey; it demands it and takes possession of it with the assurance of an inalienable right, as if it belonged to it exclusively. Mediocre people need only present themselves for the doors to open; they close *instinctively* before the superior man. Think on the quantity of mediocre men. All rakish fellows are mediocre necessarily. Do not believe in the intelligence of rakes. Enthusiasm is the recompense for simplicity, and complicated souls neither feel nor understand anything. Do not hope that mediocrity might be moved by your courage, by your efforts; here is its character: *It is naturally ruthless!* If it lets itself just once be surprised, moved, it will no longer be itself.

It has nothing improvised in its movements.

It has merely a physiognomy; it aims for seriousness. At the same time, it is aggressive, petty, irksome, narrow-minded and envious. It loves small things, small proportions, petty projects, the usual silliness, the timid ineptitudes that it is ordinarily served. It judges a man by his age, his success, his position, his fortune.

It judges him on his past and on his appearance, believing neither in the reality of men nor in their future. It has the most profound respect for those who have already published *a lot*. It weighs everything, and measures nothing. It will dare to say in front of the work of an as yet unknown man: "Now this here is glory and genius." When it sees a man overflowing with life and love, it digs a cemetery around him. In that circle there, your ardent expressions will be addressed to old men paid to watch graves, who will ask you by what right you have entered. If I insist on that unconscious cruelty that stupidity has, it is because that cruelty is unperceived by the man who practices it and by him who looks on from afar. Genius is the only suffering that finds no pity, not even from women. Women, who so voluntarily feel compassion over false grandeurs, are often merciless when it comes to real ones. They love what sparkles; they do not love what resplends.

Look at the names of those who have achieved not reputation but glory: read their story. Interrogate them; they will tell you that they have used, in order to set themselves apart from the crowd and to carve out a place for themselves, more force than was necessary to create a thousand works of art. They have spent hours that could have been beautiful and productive being subject to the punishment of a perceived injustice; they have expended the purest drops of their blood in an external and sterile fight that stopped the fecund labor of Art; discouragement has robbed them a thousand times, them and the world, of their most beautiful transports, their most youthful ardors; how many hours, which would have been hours of genius, hours of illumination, which would have shined throughout time and space, which would have produced immortal things, have been sterile hours of sadness and despondency! Now, that has perhaps been the work of the critic who remained indifferent. He has taken it upon himself to extinguish the sacred fire that he was charged with maintaining. Would that he might be buried alive!

Do you want to know just how high the critic can ascend, look at how far he can descend. Measure his possible advantages against the ravages that he can also make.

Art has its periods, its phases, its ages: one day arrives in his life when he receives full recognition, full consciousness of himself; aren't each us familiar with those admirable hours of internal light when it seems that man, in the presence and possession of himself, discovers, apperceives, for the first time, and recognizes himself? One would say that unencumbered by obstacles, and delivered of the darkness behind which he was hidden from himself, he finally enters into the freedom and joy of his being. It is a glance cast on the domains previously thought to be lost! It is a reawakening of human regard: those instants are rare and fleeting!

Most often, we are invisible to ourselves, destitute of ourselves. Man recognizes himself only in a

glimmer of lightning. Lightning interrupts the darkness, shines and goes out, and man lives with a memory, waiting for the next electrical storm.

When the glimmer passes over Art, it is the
critic that awakens. One must avenge that word: *criticism*, for the negative and restrictive meaning that has
been attached to it. It signifies discernment. Now, discernment is a work of light.

The critic is the consciousness of Art.

When Art sees and feels, when it says: "I ex-
ist, look at me," its cry for joy is the flight of the critic
who stands up and listens. Also, it lives for enthusiasm and not negation. One imagines it always turned
to face nothingness, I imagine it facing being. It is
time that it admires.

One of the prerogatives of genius is that enthusiasm, which alone has the gift of being aware of
it, has alone also the right to judge it. Mediocrity,
which is deprived of that awareness, does not apperceive in it but the negative side, the defect; it judges it
like a magistrate judges the guilty party. In the eyes
of mediocrity, genius is guilty *par excellence*; and
even if mediocrity does not find in the lessons it
knows by heart the text that condemns it, it matters
little, for it is condemned in advance by a law without
formula, made expressly for it. The great critic lives
on admiration, the little one on chicanery. Enthusiasm
is missing in this world, until the critic throws himself
at the task of rekindling it, and it becomes alive again.
Let him add his contribution to the edification of a
new youth, of the youth that the world waits for.

Youth is missing on this earth. Cadavers, grown cold, people the workshops and attics.

Debauchery has passed by there. It is what makes old men of twenty years wander through Paris, under a completely youthful sun. Now, the critic has that sublime mission of refreshing the blood of laborers and giving their youth back to them. To accomplish this task, one must have a soul. Do you believe that the artist who can create does not suffer horribly? Do you think he *never* realizes what he wishes to realize? Do you think that his work of art is necessarily a sacrifice? Do you think that the great artist wages a battle with the certainty of losing it, that he is condemned always to miss his mark, his mark being absolute beauty, which he is ordered to pursue, and forbidden from attaining, in his work? To use his life, and to ask himself whether he does not use it uselessly, sometimes to curse Art and never to be able to do without it, to begin his work and to doubt of it, to fear everything and to walk as if he feared nothing? Inspiration requires happiness. There are however men who have worked in sadness, in the night, in their pain, who have imposed silence on their cries, who have neglected their sufferings in order not to become sterile, who have produced, because they *wanted* to produce, then even when they no longer *desired*. In vain, the great artist tries to get out and about. His peers are not of this world. He must traverse the glacial terrains in solitude.

When he sees him at a distance, the small critic (I really want to acknowledge that he does not know what he does) pricks him with a thousand needles, in order to see, while playing, how many drops of blood he has left to spill.

Do you understand then the sublime task that presents itself to the true critic? He must be big enough to become a consoler. He must enter into the field of life, he must take in his hand the cold hand of him who walks alone, and with the other hand point him out to other men. He must be capable of daring enough to admire and to blacken liberally. He must shame the herd with its stupid docility towards the blind who lead it, with its stupid resistance to those who see the light of day. There where love has no place, there is nothing true, beautiful, or prolific: the character of that critic, whom one could call negative, is the absence of love. Would that the critic might awaken to a love of the infinite, for if he loves the infinite, the critic will have a view of the whole.

The first word of the mediocre man who judges someone or something always revolves around a detail, and that first word is always false, even if true. It is false by the position it occupies, by the importance given to it, by the isolation it remains in. The critic has the attitude of wishing to exclude everything that he did not say, he has the attitude of counting as everything what is nothing, and as nothing what is everything.

The great critic places himself high enough to take in, in the same view, everything and all parties. No one can judge what he does not dominate. Vulgar infatuation involves partiality. Superior enthusiasm involves impartiality, which is the judge's sacrifice. Enthusiasm gives courage, and courage has two ac-

cents. It admires what is beautiful, it blackens what is
not. What does it need then? To dare. That is the condition for everything. If you are great, it is necessary
for the critic to say so, even if you were ignorant of it
yourself and were surprised by it. He must treat you,
whatever your name or your age, as if four thousand
years had passed over your tomb. That is his duty, under pain of dishonor. If you have stolen your name, he
must say so, whoever you might be. Who then prevents us from daring, and what do we fear? Error is
not timid. Why that imbecilic respect, that respect for
nothingness? Is sovereignty of the dead an inviolable
right? Why leave the word, like a monopoly, to those
who want to prevent the blood from circulating and
the heart from beating? Is there, in favor of ineptitude
and infamy, when they are prolonged, a prescription?
Raise your voice then, you who judge: in the face of
the Art that one has made for us, raise the voice that
condemns! What good is the weapon you hold, if you
look on universal abasement calmly and collectedly?
Men who are called artists are afraid that this earth
might not have enough dirt and filth: they want to go
one better than the shames of real life by the shames
of an imaginary life that carries us along.

Reawaken then in the public the threatened
spark, the inquietude for beauty! Critics, raise your
voice and say to those men: You, artists, you, men in-
vested with such dignity and such power that your
thought becomes the bread that nourishes other men,
the blood that flows through their veins, you,
guardians of the purity of the language, you have sullied the language, you have taught your vices to your
contemporaries in order to speculate then on their de-

basement, which is your work. You who carry the name of artists and who sell your shame so dearly to men, understand your lost dignity, in order to measure, if that is at all possible, the extent of your debasement.

The great critic seeks the great poet like iron seeks a magnet. Do not ask me which of the two dominates the other; I do not assign them any rank. I wrap them in the same respect, in the same admiration. Criticism is one of the highest forms of Art. The critic fecundates the soil and proclaims the laws. He has discovered the poet; he crowns him. Both have undergone the test, both have tried, fought, suffered. Both have had the honor of exciting the same anger. Those who bow by preference before reputations have equally detested them. Let them be confused then in the same glory! Let's leave them to meet and embrace on the heights of courage and on the summits of joy. He who can say to an unknown worker: "*My child, you are a man of genius!*" deserves the immortality that he promises. To understand is to equal, said Raphael.

The field of criticism is wider than one believes generally. It is not limited to the culture of this or that tree. Nature is its domain. It must be everywhere where greatness is in peril. It has rounded the Cape of Good Hope with Vasco de Gama. All the accents, all the harmonies are permitted in his speech; the critic is permitted to love, he is permitted to sustain and support. The critic has his place near Christopher Columbus five minutes before the cry "Land! land!" rang out on the bridge of the blessed ship.

Right there is his true place; right there his labor, his destiny, his glory. Fidelity! fidelity! that there is his triumphant motto. Fidelity, it is duration conquered by enthusiasm finally. The critic must be faithful like posterity, and speak in the present the words of the future.

The critic must begin playing the role of humanity beside the man who waits, and prelude the concert that will be given over his descendants' grave. He must make names, make glories. It is he who casts rays of light. Is that palm not worth the effort to cull? As for myself, I believe that it is right that someone be there, standing and valiant, who can, after the discovery of America, having neither calumny, nor treachery, look Christopher Columbus in the face!

Jean-Jacques Rousseau

Voltaire and Rousseau have engendered two numerous and dreadful families: the one passes away before our very eyes; the other does not yet pass away. Rousseau's descendants perish today; Voltaire's do not. What gives?

For whomever does not know the truth, it all seems unintelligible; but when one holds the light up to it, it all becomes transparent, even the genealogy of error.

Voltaire lives on because he represents one thing, evil; original sin weighs down on us. No other condition is needed for the existence of Voltairians. As long as men do evil, Voltaire will be alive and well among them.

History is beautiful, when one knows how to read. Let us look at it for a moment.

Take doctrinal errors, one by one, you will not follow them for very long without seeing them decompose before your very eyes: they lose their original shape. It is pleasant to see how thwarted their founders' projects are. It is pleasant to see Luther still imposing his name on Lutherans, who have forgotten, along the way, their point of departure even. Terrible irony for the master and his disciples! The one signs with his withered name a work that is no longer his own; the others are under the influence of that name without remembering what he stood for.

All decomposes, except the truth.

But error, in order to change shape, does not change nature; there also exists in it an element that persists, that is its principle, that is the spirit of error, that is evil, for he who commits evil detests the light.

Discover a doctrinal error then, a heresy, a lie that has a learned look to it: it will dissolve, it will lose its shape, it will be replaced.

But base yourself, without forming any school, on evil itself: address, simply, without theory, the hatred that those who do evil have for the truth, and your work will be more durable.

Now, that last work is that of Voltaire: that is the secret of his longevity.

Did he form a school? No. Did he teach something? No. What is his doctrine? He does not have one. What did he do then? He blasphemed.

Now, blasphemy is within the capacity of all intelligences. Voltaire's disciple is the street urchin who goes and plays some bad joke, or the wicked fellow who goes and commits a crime. That disciple is the equal of his master if he is as wicked as him; he is his superior if he surpasses him in roguery.

That is why the progress of science, the steps that it takes towards Christianity, makes a fatal movement in the direction of doctrinal error and all systematic errors; but Voltaire resists that movement. He is so far below science that it passes over his despicable head without touching him. As it proceeds, he rots in an infernal region; he has bones to pick with it. Human thought tends to rise, like a flame: Voltaire has descended so low that he is inaccessible to thought; he is in the realm of corruption; the most peremptory argument does not touch him; he is too low to be touched; he no longer hears a human voice; he does not have such an error, he has error in the innermost sense where error is hatred: he has pure impurity. He also lasts, because impurity lasts. It is impenetrable to human speech. Words confuse Voltaire, either by the clearest intuition, or by the simplest reasoning; but the monster's hide resists bullets. He is refuted; what difference does it make? He breaks out laughing, he laughs at his defeat: he does not respond, he laughs; he is always laughing, the hideous monkey! All his life he has refuged himself behind a frightening grimace, and that is why that horrible life endures. The grimace is invincible. A man can prove the truth to another man; but how do you want to prevent a monkey from making a grimace?

Voltaire lives because he laughs. Rousseau dies because he does not laugh. Not laughing, he must speak; speaking, he must have the semblance of having something to say: from that point on, he makes himself vulnerable, he is apprehensible.

But does he have a doctrine? No. The characteristic of French philosophers is that they do not have a doctrine. Otherwise, the least among them would think themselves obliged to have one. Locke, Locke himself! Locke, if you please, has one. Rousseau does not. French philosophers, instead of doctrine, have sensations. And if by chance that word, because it is too true, does not please you, I will say, to be polite, impressions. Now, what was Rousseau's impression? It is difficult to summarize in a word those men who were unable to summarize themselves. They are hard to grasp: they can escape us. Only, if I had to summarize for myself his manner of being, I would say that it consisted in the *lachrymose apotheosis of nature*. Set out on that path, a German would have arrived at doctrinal pantheism; but Rousseau stops along the way to cry. The sentimental emotion into which his adoration for holy nature is plunged resembles a disguise that pantheism would have assumed to cross the frontier and enter into France wearing a shepherd's costume. One would say a rural pantheism that puts itself within range of a Frenchman of the eighteenth century. That pantheism is ignorant of itself even; it takes its disguise seriously. It abjures its formulas in order to speak a tender and amorous language. But I believe I can recognize it: it seems to me that it is still pantheism, even when it is too foolish to perceive it itself.

Where did that adoration of the laws of very sacred nature find its most complete expression? It is, I believe, in the *Nouvelle Héloïse*. Start a competition, convoke the universe, promise world domination to whomever might produce a more disgusting, more insipid, more pompous, emptier, more hollow, more sottish, more sentimental, more emphatic and colder work: I doubt the prize might ever be taken.

I know that I will surprise: what difference does it make? I have the duty to speak out the truth, and that duty has become a necessity for me. Will one be surprised that I think these things? No. One will be surprised that I say them. There are things that a person does not say, because nobody says them. Everyone will say them when some have begun to say them. Courage is what we lack most of all; if all men dared to speak the truths that they think, when by chance they think, the face of the world would be changed. But our cowardice prevents us from speaking the truth completely, and that makes us accomplices to those who absolutely lie. And nevertheless the future belongs only to those who dare. The mediocre man looks down from his greatness on the universal Church; he would believe he lacked respect for himself if he had let himself be penetrated by the Holy Spirit; but when a bad child lies impudently, in bad French, behold the mediocre man on his knees! and we, if we do not dare call the bad child by his name, we are lower than the mediocre man: what would you say if you read the following in a young man's manuscript:

> *Even though your mouth has spoken wisdom, the voice of nature is stronger. How to resist when it accords with the voice of the heart? Except for you, I do not see anything in this earthly sojourn that might be worthy of occupying my soul and my senses: no, without you nature means nothing to me anymore; but its dominion is in your eyes, and that is where it is invincible. It is not like that with you, celestial Julie: you are contented with charming our senses and you are*

never at war with your own. I will
grovel forever on the ground and see
you always shining in the skies... Yes,
dear lover, it seems to me that my love
is as perfect as its adorable object; all
the desires inflamed by your charms
are snuffed out in the perfection of
your soul. (Nouvelle Héloïse)

And there you have him, the great writer!
Let's pass over to the great philosopher: What would
you say about a schoolboy who wrote this:

As I approach the eternal light, its
brightness blinds me, troubles me, and
I am forced to abandon all earthly no-
tions that helped me imagine it. God is
no longer corporeal and perceptible:
the Supreme Intelligence that rules the
world is no longer the world even.
(Really?) When I hear it said that my
soul is spiritual and that God is a
Spirit, I am indignant towards that de-
basement of the divine essence, as if
God and my soul were of the same na-
ture... If he created matter, bodies,
spirits, the world, I know nothing
about it. The idea of creation confuses
me and exceeds my capacity. *God is*
eternal, without a doubt; but my spirit,
can it embrace the idea of eternity?
Why reward me in words that make no
sense? (Profession of Faith of the

Savoyard Vicar)

To make things perfect, that page was published in the *Revue des Deux-Mondes* of all places; I feel bad for it for that consecration. After having heard those things, the listener exclaims: "The good priest has spoken with a vehemence; he was moved; I was too. I thought I was hearing the divine Orpheus singing the first hymns and teaching men the cult of the gods."

Whether Rousseau makes novels with the intention of making them, or whether he makes them without knowing it, believing to speak philosophy, through his gross delirium, it is always the lacrimose apotheosis of Nature that is made to be felt in his empty phrases. Julie gives a rendezvous to her lover in a place chosen by Rousseau, who would suffice, all by himself, to characterize the eighteenth century.

> *Neither art nor the hand of men make evident their anxious efforts anywhere; one sees everywhere the tender efforts of the communal mother. It is there alone, my friend, that one is under its auspices, and where one can hear its laws.*

"They departed this morning," she adds, "that tender *father and that* incomparable *mother."*

And she jumps for joy, the charming young woman; for she is disposed to deceiving her *tender* father and that *incomparable* mother.

The sentimentality of corrupted souls erupts with each word in that cowardly and hateful J.-J. Rousseau, who never betrayed a truth without giving to it, with a contrite air, the kiss of Judas. If that man were disemboweling you, he would feel grateful to himself for having pitied you, while he's disemboweling you. Your blood spilt by him would help him admire his sensibility, for he would not see it flowing without emotion; he would grow soft with remorse, and he would despise the ingratiating individual who came to your aid calmly and without swooning.

The Savoyard vicar shares exactly, without knowing it perhaps, Julie's opinions. To establish an absolute contradiction between nature, considered perfect (*original sin does not exist*), and the supernatural order, considered as a useless absurdity, – that is the goal of that miserable man, who does not know, for all that, neither a single word of the catechism nor a term of philosophy. And that there is the goal of the entire eighteenth century. It gave semblance of respecting natural truths, which it did not respect, in order to declare them incompatible with supernatural truths, which it did not know. And that is why Rousseau dies, because he tried to establish a schism between the two lights.

The great progress of our epoch is to no longer admit the schism. The eighteenth century believed that, to be a friend of men, one had to be an enemy of God. The nineteenth century avows that whoever does not love God does not love men. The enemies of Christianity no longer disguise themselves; the cloak of philosophy, worn and torn in battles, would no longer cover their wounds. The enemies of Christianity are public enemies of all and sundry, and they do little to hide themselves. Immense progress in truth! Luther had rejected the Church: he had tried to hold onto Jesus Christ, and men let themselves be taken in; the eighteenth century rejected Jesus Christ, it made semblance to keep charity, and men let themselves be taken in; the nineteenth century, in its Satanic party, has said: "God is evil and devotion is pitiable!"

It has repudiated the natural order, like the eighteenth century had repudiated the supernatural order, like the seventeenth century had denied the Eucharist and the Church. Immense progress! for the question has been cleared up, and the nineteenth century, in the divine party, says and will say, above all: "It is time to believe everything, given everything has been repudiated."

God's cause is now man's cause.

Rousseau is dead, suffocated in the impure arms of his dreadful creation, disemboweled in his triumph by the goddess of Reason.

Paul and Virginie

O human silliness! who will fix your limits? who will
tell you: "You will go this far, you will not go any
farther? Inviolable sovereign, your measures are so
well taken that you can believe yourself in surety.
However, do not trust yourself to the rampart that you
have raised between the sun and man. Ramparts often
crumble, and Jericho has been taken."

Who among us has not spent his childhood
hearing admiration for Paul and Virginie? Who has
not been rocked in the cradle, put to sleep to the silly
murmuring of that admiration? Who among us, in the
beautiful years of his life, has not heard vauntings of
the *simplicity of that work of art and the innocence of
that heroine*? O stupidity, stupidity, I would like to
brand you with a redhot iron.

Now, if ever stupidity is execrable, it is when
it makes itself naïve and sentimental, pastoral and
tender. Old and unhealthy romance, dull, sickly
sweet, it makes one want to exact justice on all those
who resemble it. And do not think that its insignifi-
cance protects us against the spirit that dictated it; on
the contrary: man loves foolishness. The foolishness
of the writer offers the foolishness of the reader a mirror wherein the latter may contemplate and has contemplated himself, as a type. Has not Bernardin de
Saint-Pierre celebrated the charms of nature, its superiority over civilization, the sighs of love (I refer to
the little imp god)? And how do you expect that those
noble thoughts should have found echo in our hearts,

expressed as they were in a flowing, humanitarian, and sentimental prose, good for making a woman in toilette, who is otherwise bored, weep on her settee?

Eh! get up then, madame! You can be sure that in your neighborhood there are real griefs to console, real works to assist with. You can be sure that in your neighborhood someone works to make something, someone pursues a goal, someone has a will. After you have sniveled with a humanitarian philosopher, are you more disposed to assist those who work? – Only, you are no longer capable of lifting yourself up, you need another cushion for your head; and how could it be otherwise? Here is what you are asked to admire:

> *Already their mothers spoke over their cradles about their marriage, and that perspective of conjugal felicity, which charmed their own troubles, ended often by making them weep. The first one recalled that her troubles had come from having neglected hymen, and the other from having endured the laws; the first one had lifted herself up out of her condition, and the other had fallen; but they consoled themselves in thinking that one day their children, happier than them, would enjoy together, far from the cruel* prejudices *of Europe, the pleasures of love and the happiness of equality... Those women, forced by unhappiness to re-enter nature, had developed in themselves and*

> *in their children those feelings that na-*
> *ture gives in order to prevent us from*
> *falling into unhappiness.*

That needed to be cited; there will be a need to cite again. If I limited myself to describing, one might say that I exaggerate. But when I cite, one has to read. So one sees whether exaggeration is possible, and the reader of good faith will agree with me, I hope, that the word silly no longer suffices; another word is needed.

When the eighteenth century speaks of preju- dices, of nature, of feeling, or of love, I get the insipid and nauseabond taste in my mouth of a poison wrapped in spoilt jam, and I look around me, looking for a weapon to defend myself with: in the pocket of those sensitive men I imagine knives, their love leads to death and resembles it. Their sentimentality is not far from fury. When imbecilic shepherds have turned into enraged dogs, their affection, turned into rage, has not changed in nature: it has assumed its shape, that's all.

Be wary around the sentimental man: the day he is blasé over tears, remember that he will have blood. The nature that he has glorified will be com- pletely reawakened in him.

Do you want to hear some details on the edu- cation of Paul and Virginie?

> *Useless knowledge had never made*
> *them shed tears... one had never*
> *frightened them by telling them that*

God reserves terrible punishments for
ungrateful children; the only religion
they had been taught was what makes
one love it, and they did not offer long
prayers to the church...

When I said to you that it was necessary to
cite from the text –

"To what end?" you might respond perhaps;
"everyone has read *Paul and Virginie*."

"On the contrary," I will say to you, "nobody
has read it." The most unfamiliar thing in the world
are those sorts of books that everyone knows. We impose them on young people; we order them to swoon
and to be moved by those insipid stupidities.

They obey: the think they admire. That is not
all: they imitate. They imitate, quill in hand. They imitate also when they go through life. They no longer
re-read the twaddle that they were nourished on at the
age when they had need of a fortifying nourishment,
but they keep in their blood the venenous principle
that they suckled. They continue to admire, cross their
heart, with confidence, by habit, the pages they had
admired previously; they no longer remember the
pages themselves; they remember their admiration;
and they are surprised when they are forced, by a citation, to admit: "*In effect, I am not familiar with the
books that I have known since my childhood.*"

How many times have you heard *Paul and
Virginie* vaunted like *a model of style and simplicity*?
Here's Paul's declaration to his *beloved*:

> *If you go to our mothers' house, the partridge that runs towards its chicks has a less beautiful corsage and a heavier gait.*

> *"When will you come to see us again?" said some neighborhood friends to her. "At the time of sugar-cane," responded Virginie. "Your visit will be all the* sweeter *and more agreeable," responded those young women.*

What simplicity, no? Those ridiculous *précieuses* are over the top: one swoons for joy, one cannot contain oneself any longer.

The old man, that straw man, who recounts the touching story, came often to visit that innocent family: the rock from which one saw him coming was called: *The Discovery of Friendship*. One had planted there, by the goodness in one's soul, a weather vane: the one man, a knowledgable man, had written on it with Latin inscriptions! Now, Virginie, who didn't know at all how to read, not even French, *didn't approve at all of his Latin.*

> *She said that what I had put at the foot of the weather vane was too long and much too learned. "I would have preferred," she added, "'always agitated, but ever constant.'" That motto, I told her, would be more suitable for virtue. My reflection made her* blush.*"*

What purity of taste! what force! what simplicity! how conformant that is then to gentle nature! Admire the intuition! that innocent Creole, who does not know how to read, because useless knowledge has never made her shed any tears, even though she lives at a distance from the cruel prejudices of Europe, has, however, divined Marivaux![6]

Bernardin de Saint-Pierre does not admire merely Virginie's naïvety, he admires also *her lights*. And if you asked him what he means by that word, he responds to you without embarrassment:

> "*Paul and Virginie could tell the hour of the day by the shadow of the trees, the seasons by the weather when they gave their flowers and fruit. Those sweet images infuse all their conversations with the greatest of charms.*"

Do you want an example of those conversations full of charm? The example that the author gives us, I have already cited it, but I want to cite another: it is precisely the promise to pay a sweet visit at the time of sugarcane.

Some science, in fact? But that is not all; here's Virginie:

> "*My brother,*" she said, "*is the same age as the large coconut palm of the fountain, and I am that of the smaller one.*"

---

[6]Marivaux: Pierre de Marivaux (1688-1763), a French playwright and novelist with a predominant and recurring theme of love.

> *"You other Europeans (exclaims then the philosophical novelist), whose minds are filled since childhood with so many* prejudices *against happiness, you cannot conceive that nature could give so many* lights *and so many pleasures."*

Those lights blind me, to be honest, and I can see absolutely nothing.

> *Your souls (continues the writer, apostrophizing to us), circumscribed in a small sphere of human bits of knowledge, soon attain the term date of their artificial pleasures, but nature and heart are inexhaustible. Paul and Virginie had neither clocks nor almanacs.*

I revolt then finally against civilization. The almanacs that it imposes on me, and the artificial pleasures that those almanacs procure for me, have "circumscribed my soul in a small sphere of human bits of knowledge"; but I will return to the bosom of nature, and I begin by breaking my watch which corrupts me by telling the hour.

> *"Their life seemed bound to that of the trees, like that of fauns or dryads."*

I will endeavor to make mine be like that. I could become, by that process, innocent like a faun! I cannot help from remarking how poorly written that phrase is that I cite: the two "that" that it contains makes it as displeasing in its form as it is stupid in its

idea. But I realize I am affected by the cruel prejudices of Europe, and I beg the reader to wish to forget
it.

Perhaps you believe that Paul and Virginie's
lights consisted only in knowing the hour. No! Clearly they possessed that knowledge to a supereminent
degree; but I have not told all: those children of nature had still other professors than coconut palms.
Guess what tribute that Madame de La Tour, a sensitive woman who had *formerly submitted to the laws
of hymen*, brought to that innocent society.

You do not guess? that tribute, it was *a sweet
theology* which the author calls the *particular character* of that sensitive woman. But note that that theology, exempt from the cruel prejudices that you
know perhaps, taught only the portion of religion that
makes one love it (which makes sensitive souls love
it, of course). A rapprochement is offered to me,
which I don't have the strength to brush aside. Mme.
de La Tour, of lugubrious memory, had exactly the
theology of the *Revue des Deux-Mondes*, which, in its
issue of December 1, 1859, accords to Christians the
permission to choose from among God's promises.

The herd of vicious, ignorant, deaf, blind,
stupid shepherds who, in the eighteenth century,
strummed their guitar with a ferocious and sentimental air, had the mania to talk theology. The particular
character of that herd was *a sweet theology for use by
sensitive souls who ready themselves, by love of nature and of humanity, for orgy and for the slitting of
throats*.

Here is a remark that was slipped in between two parentheses. Those who have learned only that portion of religion that makes one love it, never loved it. Nonetheless, Mme. de La Tour thinks that God has mixed into a religion, otherwise respectable, useless, dangerous, and false things. It is up to us to choose. God has placed, by inadvertence, detestable things in religion that make it detested. He lacked discriminating taste, measure, reserve, delicacy: it is up to us to expurgate Christianity.

Christianity reviewed, corrected, diminished, and placed, by Mme. de La Tour, within reach of sensitive souls, does not prevent young Paul from addressing to the innocent Virginie, by way of declaration, phrases that would have resulted in sending a schoolboy into the corner:

> *"When I approach you, you ravish* all my senses. *If I touch you only with the tip of my finger,* all my body *shivers with pleasure."*

Fortunately, what's involved here is a sweet theology.

What simplicity! What utter purity and what warmth of heart! All the same, I much prefer the expression of a Breton peasant who recounted, he also, his loves: "In order to pass over a stream, the young man said, 'I had to give my hand to Marianne. I felt my blood RUN COLD. It's over, I said, I'm in love." (Historique)

Hey, nice! what do you think? The truth that

comes out of the mouth of babes? Paul, by touching Virginie with the tip of his finger, felt warmed. Etienne (that's the name of the peasant) felt his blood run cold by love. (I am referring to the little imp God.)[7]

Mme. de La Tour would not have understood the depth of that remark. Her theology *was all sentiment, like that of nature*. Do not ask the author what he meant to say: he knows nothing. What difference does it make? Don't look so close. What is certain is that despite the theology of nature Virginie *felt agitated by an unknown ill*.

> *During an* ardent night, *she* felt all the symptoms of her ill feeling redoubled. *She went outside to walk it off, in the moonlight, towards the fountain. She remembered that, in her childhood, her mother and Marguerite amused themselves bathing her with Paul in the same place, etc., etc. She caught a glimpse, in the water, of her naked arms and of her bosom, the reflections of the two palm trees planted at the time of her and her brother's birth.*

What innocence! The story of Virginie's uncomfortable nights is long: there is not, for intelligence, much interest; but I understand the utility. The old man tells Paul that when he speaks to men, it is to try *to bring them back to nature*. He wants to do something of the kind here.

---

[7]little imp God: Cupid.

Enough of this lament. What strikes me about it is the absence of view. The eighteenth century has not cast a single glance on human nature. Virginie is a sweet young girl, a bourgeoise; Paul is a stock comic character from the Opera, mediocre and sentimental. As for you, sweet theologian woman, what have I not seen and heard of your homilies! you would have inspired in me perhaps a virtue that *nature* completely and absolutely refused to me, a virtue that ought not to be unuseful to your listeners: I mean to say patience.

Convention, Fantasy, and Order

A work of art created by a second-rate artist says what the thought of the artist was. If it leaves the hands of a man of genius, it also says what the thought was; but from a much higher point of view, it says what his thought was not. For that thought, superior to all execution, rests, by its very nature, without realization. The artist has worked the marble, he has effected the realization of a certain beauty. He has disengaged latent beauty by cutting away at the shapeless matter, by destroying the block, by disengaging interior and latent forms that contain the beauty, and which were hidden behind the matter like a spark within a stone.

When he finds his execution to be perfect, that is to say without defect, the mediocre artist stops, and stops satisfied.

When he finds his execution to be alive, that is to say full of his thought, impregnated, humid, flowing with fire, the man of genius stops also, but he stops in spite of himself, sad and vanquished in his triumph.

By the cutting away of matter, he has brought his work close to his ideal; but at the moment he reaches what he was thinking, he must stop: for, with the next incision of the chisel, he would cut into his work, he would destroy it.

The matter refuses to let itself be cut anymore, and if he persists, instead of life, it is death that he will give to his creation.

So if he wishes it to be something, it is necessary that he leave it unfinished, that he be content with letting others divine, by means of what he has made, the dimension of what he had wanted to make, the scope of what he did not make.

Every work of art is a sketch. The unfinishedness of it is the mark of genius that paints in broad strokes, not expecting to terminate anything; it is his mark, his privilege, his condemnation, and his greatness.

Those who look on, say: That work is unfinished; there are some neglected details.

And the more the execution approaches the Ideal, the more the abyss that separates them appears wide and deep to the artist; the greater the number of sides of the polygon inscribed, the greater the impossibility of reaching the circle.

For the ordinary artist, whether he knows it or not, his law is formulaic. That is why he can be satisfied: his plan can be accomplished.

For the man of genius, his law is life, life and light. Also, his ocean has no shore; he knows that formula, sometimes prolific or at least useful in science, is absolutely sterile in art. Sweat must pour from his brow for the fields of life to be worked. No formula creates, nor produces; no formula suspends the cluster of grapes on the pendant vine. The habitude of genius is to substitute, in everything, life for formula.

And that is the secret of the astonishment that it causes. Those who saw it coming were persuaded, without being conscious of it, that the law was a formula, and apperceived, as they looked on, that it is life and light.

Now what appears to us, marked by lines of fire, between those on either side of it, is a line of demarcation. Among those who dispute, share, or do not share the admiration of the world, there are those who have been men of formula; the others are men of life.

Artists, for whom law is formula, are satisfied, as I have said: I add that they satisfy the public for an instant.

The formula is a recipe that it suffices to apply. There is a certain number of rules for making a good tragedy: when the rules are observed, the tragedy is made, and well made. When the rule is replaced by law, professionalism is substituted for art, mechanism is substituted for organic processes, and procedure replaces life. Now, procedure is easier than life. With a little patience one grasps the procedure. One does not grasp life except when it lets itself be grasped.

Law results from the nature of things.

The law of art is an expression of order in the domain of art.

Rule results from human convention.

It is the expression of habits, of modes substituted for laws.

There is in the human spirit a strict tendency that leads it to shake off the yoke of law, which puts it in relation with the universality of things, in order to be circumscribed within the rule, which is its work and isolates it from the universality of things. Circumscribed within the rule, man takes cover behind the formula. Replacing life with mechanics, he has replaced love by a program. Life never finds enough superabundance, the excess for it is a necessity; the mechanics are satisfied from the moment that no piece is missing. Love finds itself wanting, because it compares itself to the infinite which thought watches over from the innermost chambers of its heart, even when it sleeps. The program no longer requires anything when the conditions that it indicated are prescribed.

From there, easy success for mechanical men; their talent is within everyone's range. In order to appreciate it, one needs to be familiar with the conditions of the program that they have put together. Exempted from thinking about the infinite, they exempt their pupils, and the admiration of the latter is a recompense they have well merited.

In order to appreciate the mechanical unities of Boileau, it suffices to know how to count to three. To feel the living and organic unity that they are the parody of, there is no procedure: one must feel it; being able to count to One is not needed. In general, the mechanical rules seduce common folk by the gross allure of the vanquished difficulty. The mediocre man loves a lot of rules, just as he loves a hedge placed intentionally before a horse at gallop: he does not enjoy horses, he enjoys the ridiculous and ugly obstacle that human stupidity places in the way of that noble animal: he loves *tours de force*.

Now, the more rules, the more the mediocre man believes that there is merit in observing them. He does not perceive that those rules are equivocations, tangents by which the artist, who is incapable of creating, shamefully avoids the only difficulty worth the effort of being vanquished for, the real fight, serious, alive, and glorious, in which, seizing the matter head on and imposing on it the action of form, he extricates life and produces beauty.

The man of genius does not take the trouble to violate artificial rules: he forgets them, that is all, and the mediocre man finds him disorderly, because his view does not coincide with the law, under whose empire the man of genius is subject to.

When the man of genius is unfaithful to the truth, his fashion of offending it is not to parody it by a puerile rule, but to turn the law against itself, to precipitate himself, head first, to the bottom of the abyss, and to give the measure, by just how far he fell, of the upward flight he would have taken.

The human spirit opens up easily to convention: having hunger or thirst, when a man forgets *the law*, he tries to replace it with *a* law. All disorderly conduct aspires to create, at its very core, a certain order; for, without a certain order, disorder itself would cease to give way to the void. The disorder that refuses to return to true order constructs for itself, in order to create an illusion, a false order: the fever self-adjusts.

You have a rendezvous at six o'clock according to the clock; you arrive at six thirty, but the clock slows down by half an hour, and you are not found to be late. If you arrive at six thirty, but the clock advances by half an hour, you are found to be late by one hour: convention is a clock that marks time differently than the sun does, and which, as far as men are concerned, is right in spite of it.

Verse, that singular splendor, born of speech and music combined, furnishes us, by law and by rule, with an application that is magnificent and, by consequence, mysterious.

Speech has need of harmony, it wants to invade the domains of music without becoming confused with it. God had the complaisance of making a gift of verse to our humanity. Let's study for an instant verse in its law, verse in the rule that has been imposed on it. There are few men, among those whom one calls, perhaps ironically, cultivated spirits, for whom poetry does not invoke the most splendid joys, the most radious illuminations, and at the same time the most risible efforts, the most ungrateful drudgery that their poor adolescence had to put up with. There are two poetries then: in the hours of deliverance, the first one initiates us to it; in the hours of fatigue and stupidity, the other one takes us for its slaves; or rather there is only one poetry, and someone has parodied it. The great poet is not only a great writer. He is something more: he is minister to a mystery that I will certify.

If someone told you that there was a form of language particularly adapted to poetry and that lives on enthusiasm, you would respond maybe like this: "That form of language must be freer than others." All hindrances must fall away from it, and the poet concentrate only on his inspiration.

Now, precisely the opposite occurs. It seems that man has taken it upon himself to complicate his difficulties, to invent, for the spirit that soars, inexistent chains. Verse is a mysterious creation whose habitude alone prevents us from being surprised.

What is rhyme? A stroke of luck in appearance. If a person has never had written verse before and if someone said to you: "Begin;" without a doubt, by consulting only your reasoning, you would declare the thing not difficult, but impossible. How to hope that the phrase, without violating the thought, will naturally carry the required consonance to the end of each line; that the line will have twelve syllables, that masculine and feminine lines will alternate, and that those extraordinary exigencies of form, which ought to thwart common sense and lead to a grotesque game, a series of disjointed words, will adorn the idea with a royal mantle that would always be absent if it had not come and offered itself?

That magic of verse, does it not resemble the lamentations of the matter[8] that drags Harmony's chariot shuddering, torn to pieces doubtless, but dominated, glorified, transfigured by its power? Why, in those hours of light, when the artist sees instead of

---

[8]matter: in the sense of the "matter" of poetry.

seeks, does the rhyme come of itself, glorious and re-
splendent, in order to make the thought resplend?
Does not rhyme resemble those fortuitous encounters,
those encounters of two creatures made for each other! That agreement of persons and things least de-
signed to act in concert, does it not offer a resemblance, all the more evident the more it is concealed,
with that docility of words, of consonances which
don't dare make themselves wait when the idea calls
its servants by their name? Are they not in truth beings whose names rhyme and who meet, despite a
thousand contrary chances, to become one day an
episode in a great poem because their two types harbor the germ of a parentage that could very well be
called somewhere: Harmony?

Thus constrained and compressed in appearance by that law, poetry dilates with amplitude and
superabundance: it is the expansion of our most intimate and ardent desires. Could speech also draw from
the sacrifice a force of elevation? Thus spent in appearance, poetry is the splendor of human expression:
thus restricted in scope, it envelopes everything; thus
captive, it sings the deliverance of the spirit. No light
can grow in intensity down here on earth without
bringing with it a greater obscurity, and an apparent
contradiction. Mystery, which is at the bottom of everything, grows larger in the same proportion as beings.

Verse is condemned to the rhythm that represents the slavery to time and space. And, thanks to
that slavery, poetry breaks out in liberty, it dominates
time and space, it obliges us to feel, while shivering,

the real vicinity of the eternity that one forgets. That is why the poet has been referred to by the same name as the prophet. That is why great men have been immortalized by poetry, which makes use of the future and conflates with the past immortal things in society. On the one hand, it attains the visible, on the other the invisible, and when it presses here below on a key of the great instrument, it makes another one vibrate, the corresponding key in the invisible world.

That there is one of the forms of the law.

As for rules, read the correspondence between Boileau and Racine. It will deliver you *in flagrante delicto*. For example:

It is a question of knowing whether Homer employed, yes or no, a vulgar word. Boileau had affirmed that the Greek poet had never committed that crime and that the word *ass*,[9] as used by him, is *very noble* in Greek.

> *I have reflected, said Racine, that instead of saying that the word "ass" is, in Greek, a very noble word, you could be satisfied by saying that it has nothing vulgar about it, and that it is similar to "stag," "horse," or "sheep." The "very noble" bit seems to me rather far-fetched.*

Behold on what terrain the discussion was placed: to what degree precisely is the word "ass" noble? A little? A lot? Not at all? Completely?

---

[9]ass: donkey in this case.

One day at Mme. de Brolio's house, an interlocutor maintained that the rules were better observed in *Phèdre* by Pradon than in that by Racine. Boileau responded:

> *The peripeteia and agnition[10] must encounter each other in the same tragedy, and that is what happens in Racine's* Phèdre, *which is not at all what happens in Pradon's.*

The interlocutor interrupted Boileau to ask him what peripeteia was and agnition.

> *Ah! ah! responded Boileau, you wish to speak about rules, and you don't even know the terms. You should learn not to wish to dispute something that you have never learnt.*

Do you want to know what were, for Boileau, the sorrows of childbirth?

Read his letter dated from Auteuil, where he sends to Racine the satire of *Women*:

> *It is a work that kills me, he said, by the multitude of transitions which are, in my opinion, the most difficult to achieve in a poetic work of art.*

Perrault attacked Pindar, *whom he did not understand because of the weakness of his lights.* Boileau wants to avenge the Greek poet:

> *Perrault, he says, has treated with ri-*

---

[10]agnition: acknowledgement.

*dicule those marvelous places where
the poet, to designate a spirit entirely
outside of himself, broke sometimes by*
intentional design *the rest of his discourse.*

Do you understand? What is a great poet, if
not a charlatan, who breaks by intentional design the
flow of his discourse in order to point out a spirit entirely outside of himself?

*I thought, continued Boileau, that I
could not better justify that great poet
than by attempting to write an ode in
French in his style, that is to say full of
movements and transports, where the
spirit* appeared *more led by the demon
of poetry than guided by reason.*

Having thus taken the position of raving and
projecting madness, Boileau adds:

*In the example of ancient dithyrambic
poets, I have hazarded the boldest of
figures, to the point of speaking of the
white feather that the king ordinarily
wears in his hat, and which is like a
kind of fatal comet to his enemies, who
consider themselves lost from the moment they perceive it.*

It would be necessary to cite everything, but I
have held myself back by a sort of shame: what we
need still is enough greatness to detest what degrades

our intelligence precisely. I have spoken enough about the rules to make them known to those who might have been ignorant of them.

Thirty years ago a rather strange comedy was put on. Several insurgents had taken to task the rules, the literary conventions, and having the energy to hate them, without having the strength to dominate them, they conceived against them a fury that seemed saintly to them, a veritable fury that translated into insults. Those young people, the most famous of whom was M. Victor Hugo, had played very seriously, very doctorally, a game that consisted in taking, one by one, the habits of their predecessors and thwarting them. If one had said white, they said black. Not one among them noticed that they were subjected ironically to the constraints they claimed to deliver themselves from; for the obligation of always violating a rule was equivalent to that of always submitting to it, and constitutes another rule, which is but the exact opposite of the precedent, and which has a much greater chance of being even more irritating. They were bigoted men who had not had access to the truth. None of them was elevated to the conception of Art.

None of them had been great enough to forget himself in the face of Art. Also, all those little personalities have been forgotten, even though they had put so much stock in making a splash and some noise. Everyone was seeking to make a reputation for himself: consequently no glory was produced. If there had been a momentary *success*, the small noise that was made was for the same reason as the preceding

noise, which they had wanted to suppress. Those writers, whom one called, I have never understood why,
Romantic, had satisfied themselves and their public,
just as their predecessors had, by a procedure: the in-
verse and identical procedure.

It was the same mechanism that functioned in
a contrary sense, and as there was still a program
whose well determined conditions could be fulfilled
from beginning to end, the artist and the public could
be absolutely content, both one and the other, at curtainfall, and applaud without reservation for having
regularly revolted against all the rules without excep-
tion. There is nothing but the greatness of views that
interdicts the artist from being completely satisfied
with himself. It must be added, to be just, that that
alone brings joy also. If those readers irritated by Ho-
race and Boileau had gazed higher, instead of getting
upset, they would have laughed, and higher still, they
would have wept.

The ridiculous battle between the classics and
the Romantics has been a melee of myopic midgets
fighting in the dark in order to take hold of an unknown prey located on a mountain, out of range of
their arms and eyes, the prey of eagles. Boileau and
Victor Hugo having been vanquished not one by the
other, but one in spite of the other, and each of them
by himself, the combat ended for want of combatants:
they were both drowned in the unhealthy deluge of
their vain words, like two flies in a glass of water,
without either of them having thought to resolve, or
even to pose, the question. Instead of simply forgetting *the poetic arts*, the school of 1830 had the debili-

ty of execrating it; instead of giving deliverance to the world, it offered to the audience in the orchestra the comic spectacle of a vengeance.

What characterizes the two systems is the limit. Now, the limit is also inexorable in the new system as in the old. Every system, by the very fact that it is a system, believes that it is not enough to speak as one thinks. It adds to speech other obligations than its natural obligations. It desires beauty for it, which comes elsewhere than from the nature of things. The greatest misfortune that could happen to style is for it to be admired, independently of the ideal that it expresses: and the system always condemns it to that dishonorable misfortune. The system orders it to be noble on the one hand, familiar on the other, etc., etc., and conceals from it its glory, its true and innermost splendor, which is faithfulness.

New legislators (they have earned that name) have replaced convention with fantasy, that is to say with itself; for convention is the fantasy of several men. Fantasy is the convention that a man makes with himself.

Convention and fantasy, having nothing to do with the infinite, are always content with themselves and please the public with an attitude of novelty, which fantasy carries proudly and which convention dissimulates under a false attitude of old age. But the illusory satisfaction they both produce leaves behind an emptiness that only truth can fill.

Man is so small that he takes pleasure in himself; but he is so big that he is not satisfied except in

God. The school principal wants to be master: he imposes *his* system. The disciple of truth wants to be servant: he accepts the law that he has not made. Now, he who wants to be master mistakes his greatness and his lack of ambition, for he mistakes his end goal, which is his glory, by taking himself for the goal.

The role of servant is only great enough for man. Let God give us men of genius then, ambitious enough to forget themselves, great enough to be humble, humble enough to be great, which restitutes to things their lost majesty.

Among common men, some believe that poetry is an exercise brought to completion by means of a formula: others take it for a madness that has disorder itself for a condition, which is unsettled in its essence; now, here is the truth. Poetry and music, which thrive on love, have their roots in mathematics, inflexible and absolutely exact, as if love and order, which sometimes seem like enemies to us, assume I do not know what affectation to proclaim themselves united in those lofty manifestations of themselves.

Art

In view of this subject, which has occupied my life, and which is one with me, I would like to be able to say everything about it in one word. But Art, when it enters among us, is subject to the law of succession: it becomes divided; it admits the *before*, the *after*: it assumes different forms. When speaking about it, one must obey the same necessity, enter into the same harmonies.

Art is the perceptible expression of beauty.

It is, in the natural order, the manifestation of the ideal.

Art has no reason for being among us: it is one of the natural gifts of God.

How will it manage to penetrate our land of exile?

Time and space guard the barriers of that world and grab everything that tries to enter. Nothing escapes their grasp. Without violating unity, Art will soften the immense and complacent splendors in order to accommodate them to our human speciality.

Its first act will be a concession, a sacrifice. We saw later that sacrifice is the essence of speech. Sound is born merely to die, and does not take possession of itself except to give of itself.

Art is divided in order to appear.

Forced to submit to time and space, it asks

them for their assistance in order to remain beautiful among them. Time loans it speech, space loans it light.

Speech and light are Art's two ministers.

Arithmetic expresses the laws of time, geometry the laws of space. Arithmetic gives birth to poetry and music in the world of art, idea's ministers in the department of time. It is time that sets the measure. Their condition is rhythm.

Geometry launches architecture, sculpture, and painting into the ideal world, idea's ministers in the department of space; it is space that gives them their proportions.

The forms of Art that objectify thought, with respect to the phenomena of time, have speech for their minister.

The forms of Art that objectify thought, with respect to the phenomena of space, have light for their ministers.

Speech and light strike me by their hidden similitudes. Speech is the splendor of the invisible world; light is the splendor of the visible world. Through speech, creation makes light: it explains its splendors to our intelligences. Through light, creation makes speech: it explains the glory of the Creator. The heavens would be mute, destitute of light, as man would be mute, destitute of speech. Human speech explains the beauty of that creation which is revealed to us by light; through speech and light, the visible and invisible are brought together and glorify each other. They speak, they praise, they sing: they sing their love in the joy of their beauty. Speech and light are the same friends and the same enemies.

Light exposes the visible world to admiration and intelligence, speech makes the world visible in the service of intelligence. Both are imponderable, mysterious. Both belong to each other and to every-thing, without division, with diminution. Both tra-verse, touching and penetrating, the most abject bod-ies without sullying their rays. Both reflect each oth-er: the echo sends back speech, the mirror sends back light. Let light penetrate a drop of water, it will turn it into a pearl. Let speech penetrate a dead intelligence. God knows what colors he will see it emit. Warmth follows light, and love follows speech.

Speech and light both chase away phantoms. Both unveil. Do you want to know the value of that object? Give it a name. Do you want to unmask that criminal? Name him.

Crime flees speech as it flees light, and deceit is an obscurity.

The name expresses the moral being just as light permits perception of the material object.

Speech *clarifies* what it names. Light *defines* what it shows. Both distinguish, determine. Both fly off and disappear: radiant by nature, both hide in or-der to act, the one at the bottom of souls, the other at the back of bodies, and manifest their presence only as long as they can find matter for their activity: both assimilate what is grasped, subjugating everything to

themselves, not subjugating themselves to anything.
They discern their prey, like an eagle, from the mountain tops, swooping down on it, devouring it, renew-
ing it, then taking flight again, escaping, by their rapidity, any enslavement; but they subsist, by their
communicated splendor, in the body they have taken
possession of. When they are deposited, like a seed,
somewhere, their active and unperceived presence demands a shock for them to wake up again. Shocked,
they burst out; they shine then and they communicate
themselves without diminishing. The day that man,
surprising light at work, invented *a mirror that remembers*, he discovered through photography the law
of speech. Permanent and faithful there where it is attached, but mysterious in its operations, speech obtained residence, often in the soul, but only shows itself under certain conditions.

Man, who received the gift of speech, is particularly moved by the beauty of light. Light is so evident a symbol that its name is applied as often to invisible as to visible light. In artistic creation, at the
precise instant, at that admirable instant when it expresses the beauty that he is thinking, the artist feels
himself penetrated by an invisible light, a warm light
and a vivifying light, which will give him speech.
Full of his thought, possessed by its type, he feels
something moving inside himself. Those are the
words that are born, luminous and ardent, in his mind.
They model themselves on the thought, embellish
themselves by its beauty, resplend with its splendor.

Thought is so beautiful, when he contemplates
it, not yet realized, in its unity and in its integrity,

without having dirtied his hands in multiple material, in order to certify it, one more time, as incapable, insufficient, and however useful to his plans! Writer, painter, or sculptor, when he takes into his trembling hands the instrument that realizes, he listens to thought, readies its minister, *works*, contemplates his work and finds it imperfect. The problem is that he has not realized his ideal. The ideal demands more, and having no more to give, the artist, empty-handed, weeps and asks pardon. He has lowered his thought, in order to give it a face. He has put a limit on it, he has determined it. He has renounced the immensity in which he contemplates it. He has made an attempt on the life of his ideal.

The rising of the sun is the triumph of light in this world. Creation reappears. Let there be light, and look! That magnificence is the symbolic and mysterious reflection of some invisible and spiritual harmony that wants to let itself be symbolized by color.

The rising of the sun resembles the creation of the world; it is the face of it! Does it not marvelously resemble the rising of speech in the artist's soul? Sometimes *it is midnight in the soul*, and at that hour then man can do nothing. But, all of a sudden, he sees his thought resplend: it is speech that rises. His thought was latent, it becomes luminous: it was, for man, as if it did not exist. It receives the consciousness and splendor of its truth. It feels alive, because it speaks.

Speech, like light, rises slowly on the horizon. At first it is a glimmer, then a burst of day. Just as at the rising of the sun, ferocious beasts return to their

lair, passions conceal themselves, feeling ashamed
when speech rises, illuminates, and inundates. Then a
cloud troubles speech in the soul, like light in the sky;
but they play together in that inferior difficulty; they
oscillate and break out into divers displays that embellish the sky and earth with more varied, more
abundant, and richer splendors. Finally, full daylight
appears and warmth arrives. The laborer digs his fur-
row: the torn fields are exposed to the sky's influences, and the earth bears its fruit.

Let us contemplate finally the splendor of
Harmony. We say: that melody is beautiful and, in a
painting, that face is beautiful.

Harmony, which is the beauty of speech, has
its roots in rhythm, that is to say, in numbers.

Beauty, with a capital B, which is the harmony of Form and the splendor of Art exposed to the
Light, has, like another harmony, its root in numbers;
for Beauty resides essentially in the Angle, and the
Angle can be resolved to a number.

One must not be surprised if art, such as it is,
practiced by the majority of those who call themselves artists, is so hideous and so ridiculous a mas-
querade. The depth of the fall is measured by the
height that he who falls had obtained! How indignant,
if that's how things are, how indignant must the artist
be? Think about Art and judge for yourself! Guess
how far he falls, he who had to climb that high, when,
instead of climbing, he descends. He descends be-
neath the ground; for he must dominate it. He debases
and obscures, if that is even possible, material reali-

ties, for it was he who had to transfigure them. Moving along, head lowered, and condemned by the nature of things, in search of a certain ideal, he asks it of the mud, the only perspective he has available in his line of sight.

To comprehend what he is, without however looking at him, let's see what the artist can be. Let's forget his fall, let's not measure him anymore except by the height he could obtain. It must give him some air for his soul. Art, in a certain measure and at a certain moment, is the force that breaks open the vault of the subterranean cavity wherein we are suffocating. What lever does he have at his disposal then? What masses are at his service? Speech, music. O feeble things! A little air ploded by fleshly lips.

Poor little grains of incense, invisible majesties, how powerful you are! You move the earth, and the sky listens to you. In the solemn instants when we belong to you, the soul has some air: it respires, it gains consciousness of itself. It says: Yes, my God, I am great and I had forgotten it. Through you, the human soul tastes the first fruits of its deliverance. It is surprised then by its habitual oblivions; it is surprised for not having always remembered what it remembers instantly. The accidental light uncovers for it the depth of ordinary darknesses! In the face of that re-awakening, it no longer comprehends anything but itself, and does not remember its sleep except to be astonished by it. It is astonished to have been able to forget types, to the point of being buried in accidents, in ugliness. A thick and heavy door, the door to our prison, masks our

great love; it hides it from us sometimes until we remember. But suddenly the horizon appears, broad and
profound, distant, charged with glimmers, streaming
with fire. Carried away by speech and light, lifted on
the crossed wings of two eagles, Art has passed, it has
traversed, it has destroyed: the wall moves aside in-
stantaneously, broken by imponderable power, by the
vapor of incense, like a thick cloud split open by
lightning...

Asia, Greece, Rome

Asia, Greece, Rome (the Rome of Romulus). Speculation, science, and formula: those three words translate the three concepts of human knowledge that our
humanity developed formerly, three aspects by which
it has evaluated the works of its intelligence. When
those three points of view are given to contradictions,
then contradiction reigns in the domains of human intelligence; when those three ideas exist at war, art is
the expression of that war.

If peace reigned over those domains, at least
insofar as this world is concerned, art would be the
expression of peace.

Let's cast a glance at ancient history.

What do we see?

Asia, to start. Asia, that is to say with an open
eye. Everywhere where traditions have not been kept
intact, truth blends with error. But all thought, true or
false, that comes from ancient Asia has the character
of a observed spectacle, and not that of a found formula. Error and truth, which come from Asia, if they
are absolutely different, insofar as the one is truth and
the other is error, both have one character in common,
and to define that character I cede word to Joseph de
Maistre. I need to hear now that friendly voice, that
powerful voice. I need to hear him speak to me of the
Orient:

"Asia," he says, *"having been the the-*

ater of the greatest marvels, it is not surprising that its peoples have preserved a penchant for the marvelous, stronger than what is natural for man in general, and which each can recognize in himself. Because of which, it happens that they have always shown so little taste and talent for our sciences of conclusion. One might say that they still remember primitive knowledge and the era of intuition. Does an enchained eagle ask a hot-air balloon to rise into the air? No; it asks only that its ties be broken. And who knows whether those peoples are not destined to contemplate scenes that will be refused to the quibbler-genius of Europe? Whatever might be the case, consider, I entreat you, that it is impossible to think of modern science, without seeing it constantly surrounded by all the machines of the mind and all the methods of art. Under the skimpy habit of the North, its head lost in the curls of a false head of hair, arms filled with books and instruments of all kinds, pale complexion for vigils and hard work, it drags itself sullied by ink and panting onto the path of truth, always lowering its forehead furrowed by algebra towards the earth. There is nothing like it in high antiquity. As much as it is possible for us to perceive the science of primitive times at so enormous a distance, one always sees it free and isolated, flying more than walking and presenting in all its person something aerial and supernatural. It abandons to the wind its hair that escapes from under an Oriental miter, the ephod covers its breast lifted up by inspiration; it looks at the sky only, its contemptuous foot seems to touch the earth only in order to leave it, etc."

(Let's start a parenthetical comment here. Nothing is more annoying than copying; eh, well! the page I have just transcribed is not only agreeable to read, it is *agreeable to copy*. Glory to genius!)

Let's continue, I have not quit my subject.

The Spirit of the Orient, it is Art, that is to say repose. Oriental science, it is esthetics.

The spirit of Greece, it is science, that is to say work. Greece does not contemplate; it judges, it compares, it measures. Its instrument is the caliper. The measure! Greece is all contained in that word. All its beauty is in proportion. The sublime is unknown to it, for the sublime is what eludes, not the measure (one would need for that to escape the laws of creation, and outside the law one would attain only disorder), but the common measure, the ordinary measure, the measure such as men are accustomed to determine it. The sublime is a quantity incommensurable with our habits, because it touches a much higher habitude. It is a number that we do not mention in the accounts of our business affairs, it is an unknown angle.

The Greek angle is the habitual angle. Greek architecture is the work of that angle. It is not the architecture of speculation, it is that of science.

Greek sculpture is the straight line, the line easy to measure. Its beauty is not violated, as the Germans have said, even in sorrow. See Niobe. I would add that that same beauty is not *violated* by the sublime either: see Venus de Milo.

Greek tragedy, it is Greek sculpture in motion: the actors wear a mask and speak through a megaphone.

Egyptian sculpture is hieratic; its character, essentially typical and symbolic, allows it not to represent human form, but always makes it represent an idea. There is never a man to be shown, it is always something sacred and mysterious that must be comprehended. The hieroglyphic character is always there: the language of the Orient, it is the symbol.

In Greece, the statuary is no longer directly at the service of religion, it is at the service of nationality; it no longer expresses mystery, it does not express the individual even, it expresses the type. If it represents a god, it is that god of Olympus who is neither hidden, nor terrible, nor grandiose, that god who is a Greek, and whom one rubs elbows with while promenading into its domains, into human domains.

The more antique the art, the more it expresses a general idea.

Greece snatches it from the sanctuary where the Orient had put it, and places it on the altar of human beauty, represented exclusively by Greek beauty.

We are going to see it now on the altar of the fatherland.

For Greece had succeeded Asia, but Rome, the Rome of Romulus, the Rome of the wolf, is the one who lies in wait for its prey, and its prey is the world; but the world of that time, it was really Greece that represented it.

The day when Rome devoured Greece, formula devoured science.

As certainly as the Orient is speculative and Greece is scientific, Rome is formulary: look at its laws. It sends someone to copy in Athens, and it writes the twelve Tablets under strange dictation. Its generals lift from Greece its works of art but oblige those who transport them to furnish similar works, if they damage the originals. That Rome believed in the power of recipes. It always acted in the same way, suffocating coldly in its marble arms the aspirations of the vanquished, and regulated what it had conquered.

Look at its art: it imitates, it copies, it reduces to a formula. Its literature is a period of Greek literature, and that period is one of formulas.

It was quite necessary, in the final analysis, that the conquered universe should serve for something. Eh, well! it would furnish the formula. One rummages among the vanquished; they have beauty, one takes it, or at least one believes one takes it. The victor believes he does them too much honor by borrowing something from them, them, the inferior races, who did not know how to defend themselves; it will demand their secrets from them, but their secrets are not to be taken, they are given: they are given to friends, for the secret is life's marrow, and when the enemy wants to take them, he snatches only their formula. Greece's secret was beauty; Rome, in despoiling the vanquished, thought it was taking that beauty: but when it opened its victorious hands to show its prey to the world, it was a skeleton that it displayed; it held only the skeleton of the Venus de Milo.

It had only the formula of beautiful proportions.

In general, he who wants to copy elegance attains grossness. That cult of proportions, which made the splendor of Athens, became for Rome the cult of mass and the adoration of solidity. Greece had adored beauty. Rome adored only force.

It is a magnificent spectacle to see speculation, science, and formula grappling amongst themselves, adorned under these three names: Asia, Greece, and Rome. Bizarre thing! Victory has always gone down hill.

Greece vanquished Asia at Troy. It recounted its victory, and we have the *Iliad*.

Rome vanquished Greece, the day that it laid its first stone. Its foundation is its victory. It recounted its victory, and we have the *Aeneid*.

But was I not mistaken when I said that Homer had recounted the victory of Greece over Asia?

I was mistaken! Homer recounted the battle, but Homer was one of the vanquished. Homer loved Hector, Homer sang his oriental preferences in Greek; Homer recounted the battle, but his courage failed him when recounting the victory; he left that difficulty to Virgil, to the Roman Virgil, to Virgil whose hand did not tremble. You believe perhaps that Virgil wept over Ilion, because, in the *Aeneid*, it is Aeneas who speaks? Disabuse yourself: it was the Greek Homer who wept over Ilion: it was he who wept with Hector, foretelling and predicting with him that the walls of Troy were going to tumble: it was he who wept when he thought those things χατα φρενα χαι χατα Φυμον; but Aeneas, Virgil's Aeneas, no longer remembers his oriental origins; with a dry and gay eye, he sees Priam's city fall and burn, because that prepares for the Battle of Pharsalus, and Mæcenas and Virgil. He is Juno's accomplice, and his hand does not tremble.

When it conquered Greece, Rome knew that it conquered the world. Some friends of the old mystery still remained in the Occident. The druidical forests were still standing, the mistletoe of oaks was still there, like a final protestation. But Rome felt itself the stronger; from the moment it had vanquished science and ruse, Greece and Carthage, it understood that the forests of Gaul would illuminate their depth before its armies, that the sacred oaks would fall under the axe of its soldiers, and that the military formula would get the better of humanity.

Statuary, in Rome, is no longer hieratic as in Egypt, nor beautiful as in Greece: it is patriotic. It is a portrait, and that portrait is the portrait of Rome or the portrait of a Roman. It is neither a god, nor a type, it is an individual, a soldier; it is, if you wish, Jupiter Stator. How Roman that epithet! How perfect that God for Rome! That devouring Rome, having conquered the world, wants to conquer intelligences; it wants to be at one and the same time the center of the visible world and the center of the invisible world, to dominate at the same time Europe, Asia, Africa, and at the same time religion, science, and art. The Roman's religion, it was Rome. It was Rome one had to serve, Rome one had to love, Rome one had to adore. What was the point in painting or singing anything else? Rome absorbed the Roman in its lifeless unity, and life, hunted, had no refuge; the temples were invaded as were the houses by that terrible fatherland; neither religion, nor literature, nor family, nothing escaped Rome's stranglehold: Rome spread out over the universe, over thought, over the soul, like one immense formula, stiff like a formula, calm, inflexible, and inexorable.

A day came when the great machine cracked. The world, put to sleep, was awakened by the cracking sound. The worn out gearwheels no longer functioned. The Rome of the wolf, for a long time already, had no more blood in its veins, and that movement of rotation on itself, a little like life, which it preserved by habit, was going to be snuffed out by lassitude.

The formula had provided for its career. It no longer sufficed.

For quite a long time now, the Orient no longer dominated the Occident. The Jewish people had guarded the depot in spite of everything, so as to attest God, by the very singularity of their faith. But the Orient was conquered. Extraordinary thing! The Homer of the *Odyssey* is already no longer the Homer of the *Iliad*. The Iliad attests, as I just now said, the oriental preferences of that Greek who wept for Troy, and who one might say was born in Priam's palace. But in the *Odyssey*, the Greek appeared. The *Odyssey* is less lofty and more learned than the *Iliad*. One might believe sometimes to recognize in the style of the *Iliad* a descendent of Chaldean shepherds; the *Odyssey*'s style betrays an ancestor of Pericles. By leading Ulysses back to Ithaca, one might say that Homer was reconciled with the things of the Occident. Later, the king of Macedonia dominates Asia; India is terrified, the earth falls silent before him; Greek civilization imposes itself on the extremities of the world; the Asian seas, if they had held on to something of the perfume of ancient days, at the hour when Alexander's vessels traversed them for the first time, the Asian seas must have been surprised to see science passing by.

A few days later, that very proud science was yoked to the chariot of a Roman soldier, and a few days later Rome fell in putrefaction.

But, around that time, on a December night, the kings of Orientile were traveling, guided by a star, and on that same night the shepherds heard the angels singing: "Glory to God in the highest, peace on earth and goodwill to all men!"

And Rome, while playing, prepares in its arenas the future's harvest. The seed that never perishes was confided to the earth. The blood of martyrs was going to germinate.

Now, what is our task? What is the task of the nineteenth century? Its task is to feel and to proclaim with great accord, the accord of speculation, what I will now call art; the accord of art, science, and formula, accord of the Orient and the Occident. That harmony, which exists, it is a matter of making it resonate, as much as the vibrations of the terrestrial atmosphere contain it, over the surface of the inhabited globe. By perhaps the most bizarre of ignorances, men have come to believe that human knowledge, human works, are contradictory to themselves, the ones having at bottom truth, the others beauty; and others still, not having a bottom at all, and having the right not to have one.

At the basis of that deliriousness, truth and beauty, mutual enemies, fight each other in the void. Men admit sometimes that order is good in science, but they are persuaded that disorder is the condition of art. Some think that evil is the domain of art, that the artist, to be an artist, must live outside the law, and that what is beautiful is sin.

Men, having regarded as contradictory the things that ought to be united, have become contrary to one another, those who should be united. The Occident has become the enemy of the Orient just as work

has become the enemy of repose! Also, work and repose tend to both bottom out in infecund fatigue, a
monotonous nightmare that replaces at the same time
sleep and vigil.

Make way for life finally! Make way for light!
Make way for peace!

To formula responds law, to science responds
truth, to art responds beauty. Order responds to everything and nothing contradicts anything. Never does a
being contradict itself, nor turn against itself. It is
nothingness that betrays itself.

Let's put the truths of natural order under the
protection of the truths of supernatural order. Let's
listen, like shepherds, to the song of angels, the song
of glory, and the song of peace! Let's put our human
flags, which wave between our fingers from the moment the wind rises, under the protection and under
the shadow of the standard that does not wave. The
Rome of death had given asylum to all the gods. The
Rome of life gives asylum to all the saints. May art,
may science, may formula never attempt anything
against God who Is! May the Orient and the Occident,
turned to face each another finally, embrace already
as tightly as they can before the complete embrace, as
tightly as they can before the angel has proclaimed
the end of time! May the Orient and the Occident,
contemplating simultaneously, with their eyes open,
the eastern gate, which Rome proclaims to be immac-
ulate, Mary, the Holy Virgin, – may they embrace in
natural beliefs, in supernatural beliefs, in the immense
arms of the Church, opened wide like those of the
Crucified!

Voltaire the Critic

> Sources of criticism according to Voltaire. – His
> opinion on the nature of beauty. – Plato, the toad, and
> the devil. – Envy, according to Voltaire, is the mother
> of art. – The connoisseur in poetry, music, and medals.
> – Academies and bookstores. – Arts and beaux-arts. –
> For Voltaire, all art is tragedy. Shakespeare is little
> more than Harlequin. – Iphigenia in Aulis. – The taste
> for gifts, according to Voltaire, inspired Racine, and
> vexation, Corneille. – Genius and talent. – Taste,
> according to Voltaire. – Matter and thought.

Here is an interesting and facile experiment that I recommend to you: address yourself to a Voltairian and
cite some phrases by Voltaire to him. In his quality as
a Voltairian, he should, you would think, admire
them, or, if he does not admire Voltaire, he is not
Voltairian. Try it, I tell you: cite Voltaire to a
Voltairian, the Voltairian will be indignant...

      With Voltaire apparently?

      No! With you.

      Here's the secret, for there is a secret in what
follows: Voltaire exists only on the condition of his
being inexplicable. Also, his adorers drop his name
nonstop, but they never cite him: and if you cite him
to them, they get upset; for, even though they can always be dropping his name, it must be that they can
never look at him. By demasking him, you remove
their last power, which is public ignorance; for, pay
attention to this, to be a Voltairian is not to love

Voltaire (nobody loves Voltaire), it is to detest God.

But if you show Voltaire in his nudity, his friends grow irritated, because they lose the right to write on their standards a symbol that becomes too compromising. One would need to keep Voltaire in a cloud in order always to prevail by his authority. The Israelites were afraid to see the face of their God and die because it was too beautiful to be supported; the Voltairians are afraid to see the face of their god and die because it is too ugly to be supported.

* * *

I am not going to say everything about Voltaire. The task would take much too long, and besides it has already been done in great part. If I say to you that Voltaire is the enemy of God, I tell you something evident. If I tell you that he is the enemy of humanity, I tell you something that begins to be evident. But if I tell you that Voltaire is the enemy of art, the personal enemy of beauty, the most obstinate defender of the most absurd prejudices, I tell you a thing that will be evident one day, but which today is unknown to the point of seeming paradoxical.

Voltaire passed for an oracle of taste: it is the oracle of taste that we are going to interrogate.

One often asks him what he thinks of Jesus Christ: we know his response. But one never asks him what he thinks of art. We are going to ask him, and we will hear his response. We will examine then only the literary critic in him.

* * *

I open the *Philosophical Dictionary* to the entry on "Criticism." We are going to ask Voltaire what is, according to him, the philosophical meaning, the most elevated meaning, of criticism.

> *The definition of* Criticism, *by M. de Marmontel, in the Encyclopedia, is so good that it would be unpardonable of me to give a new one here, unless it treated of a completely different matter under the same heading. What we intend here is the criticism born of envy, as ancient as the human race. About 3000 years ago, Hesiod said: "the potter has envy of the potter, the blacksmith of the blacksmith, the musician of the musician."*

If that does not make your head spin on those heights, if vertigo does not seize you, keep going, and do not forget that I am reading to you from a *Philosophical Dictionary*:

> *One has seen, said Voltaire, among modern nations who cultivate letters, people who established themselves as critics by profession, just as one has invented tongue inspectors of pigs to examine whether those animals that are led to market are not ill. The tongue inspectors of literature do not find any author fully healthy: they make a reckoning two or three times a month of all the reigning illnesses, of bad verse composed in the capital and*

in the provinces, of the insipid novels
that Europe is inundated with; new
systems of physique, secrets to kill
bugs by. They earn some money at that
profession, above all when they speak
badly of good works, and well of bad
ones. They can be compared to toads
that serve to suck the venom from the
earth and to communicate it to those
who touch them.

Two pages later, Voltaire declares that "critic" means good judge and *that one must be a Quintilian[11] to dare judge the works of others, or at least one must write like Bayle,[12] who has few imitators.*

There we have it, the extent of Voltaire's philosophical conception. The critic must imitate Quintilian and Bayle, or resemble a tongue inspector of pigs.

Let's open the same dictionary, which is called Philosophical, to the word "Eloquence." Voltaire repeats the old distinction of simple genre, tempered genre, and sublime genre. But here is what belongs to him exclusively; see with what ingenious and profound remark he rejuvenates that classification which is already a bit old:

The simple genre, says Voltaire, can

[11]Quintilian: Marcus Fabius Quintilianus (35-100 AD), a Roman teacher and rhetorician, whose *Institutio Oratoria* was an important work of literary criticism.

[12]Bayle: Pierre Bayle (1647-1706 AD), a French lexicographer whose *Historical and Critical Dictionary* was influential.

have only to do with powerful interests
treated in a great assembly.

That discovery has its importance. Do not try to be sublime then if you have two or three thousand listeners. I wish Voltaire had fixed the exact number for it. The vagueness of it leaves a cloud in my mind. Nevertheless, I owe him some recognition. I had thought until today that the *fiat lux* was sublime in Moses; but given that word had not been pronounced in full parliament, and because he who pronounced it was the only one around to hear it spoken, it belongs only to the simple genre, which is the opposite of the sublime genre; for, as you know, to be sublime, the first condition is not to be simple.

Those errors have an advantage. They make the greatness of Art stand out, by parodying it. They inspire the need to repose in contemplation of majesty. They precipitate you to the truth by the distance they inspire you to take from them. When one is condemned for one instant to look at an ape, one must needs look at man. O holy truth that men do not dare tell! Never however will you lose your rights, and Voltaire will remain what he is.

I am going to cite, and cite a lot. I will leave the floor to him. I want only to notice, indicate, uncover. Only, let him appear, and I am certain that he will embarrass his partisans. Against him, there is no possible justice but that of photography.

I open the *Philosophical Dictionary* to the entry on "Beauty." Expect anything; I defy you to guess what you are about to read.

One will be curious perhaps, said Voltaire, to know how a Greek spoke about beauty more than two thousand years ago. According to Plato, when a man initiated into secret mysteries sees a beautiful face, or some incorporeal beauty, he feels at first a secret shuddering and I do not know what respectful fear: when the influence of beauty enters his soul through his eyes, he grows warm: the wings of his soul are moistened (for the soul had wings formerly).

I cite again:

I want to believe, continues Voltaire, that nothing is more beautiful than that discourse by Plato; but he does not give us any very clear ideas as to the nature of beauty. Ask a toad what beauty is, great beauty, the To χαλον: he will respond that it is his female toad, with her two big round eyes sticking out of her little head, a large, flat mouth, yellow belly, brown back.

Go ask the devil: he will tell you that beauty is a pair of horns, four claws, and a tail. Consult the philosophers: they will responded to you in gibberish; they need something similar to an archetype of beauty – in essence, a To χαλον.

Voltaire has gotten to the point now of being unable to distinguish between the absolute and the relative in admiration anymore. His irreflection, his ignorance in the most elementary metaphysical facts, have the last word in those lines.

The opinion of a toad and that of a devil, compared to that of Plato, are chilling frivolities, which do not have the merit even of being amusing. Perhaps he was mistaken, I imagine; but one should maintain a certain dignity in one's error. One should be mistaken like a man who has intelligence.

* * *

Do you want to see to the very bottom of the soul where the expressions I just cited come from? Do you want to know the man who was able to speak about beauty in those terms. We are talking about art, we are talking about beauty; but as we are also talking about Voltaire, do you know what word I am now about to turn to in the *Philosophical Dictionary*? I am going to turn to the word "Envy." We will find our man's secret there:

Listen to this!

Mandeville, he said, believes that without envy the arts would be mediocrely cultivated; and that Raphael would not have been a great painter if he had not been envious of Michelangelo. Mandeville has perhaps mistaken emulation for envy. Perhaps also emulation is nothing more than

envy which keeps within the limits of
decency.

I admire the roundabout way in which Voltaire borrows an unfamiliar name to pawn off what he
wants to say. But I admire even more the justice that
punishes men of that type by obliging them to betray
themselves. If great thoughts come from a great heart,
the opposite is also true. Voltaire went looking for the
source of beauty, the motive for artistic creation: he
found envy. I thank him for having given us an idea
of his measure. How was his soul made, he who was
able to confuse the transport of inspiration with the
scheming of envy? God knows the happiness of the
great artist when he encounters a great artist! He becomes complete in him. The mark of a great artist is
shared joy.

Inhabiting the ordinarily solitary heights, if he
encounters in his domains another isolated person, he
loves him with a greatness that other men do not even
suspect. I appeal to those who know these things, and
I denounce Voltaire to them. Envy, he said just now,
is the first motive of the critic; envy, he now says, is
the first motive of art. Envy, always envy! What kind
of artist is he who is an artist by envy! The sign of
narrow, egotistical beings without intelligence and
without a heart; the mark of base souls, that impotent
rage, both ugly and irksome: envy!

I recognize in that theory of Art the man who
said this:

It is curiosity alone that makes one
run to the shore to see a vessel the

tempest has capsized. That happened to me once, and I swear to you that MY PLEASURE, mixed with disquietude and malaise, was not at all the fruit of my reflection: I was curious and sensitive.

I add no commentary. I come back rather quickly to the critic, whom I never left, for what it is worth, because critical sense is in the soul.

* * *

The connoisseur in music, in painting, in architecture, in poetry, in coins, says Voltaire, experiences sensations that common men do not even think of. The very pleasure of discovering a defect strokes him, and makes him feel beauty more vividly. It is the advantage of good views over bad. The man of taste is shocked by Raphael's mean draperies but admires the noble correction in the drawing. He has the pleasure of noticing that Laocoön's children have no proportion with respect to the size of their father; but as a group they make him shiver, while other spectators remain calm.

The celebrated sculptor, a man of letters and genius, who made the colossal statue of Peter I of St. Petersburg, criticizes with reason the attitude of Moses by Michelangelo, with his small, tight jacket that is not even the

oriental costume; at the same time, he
is ecstatic while contemplating the at-
titude of the head."

Do you not envy those happy connoisseurs
who have the pleasure of perceiving so many defects,
there where others would have only the vulgar joy of
admiration? And do you not have pity for those poor
folk who, standing before Moses, would forget his little jacket, and would not ask themselves even, on
first sight, if it is too tight? But also, the famous sculptor who rose to that great observation was a man *of*
letters and genius. The juxtaposition of those two
words is excellent, but does not equal however him
whom I want to point out to you: the connoisseur of
music, poetry, and coins.

The comparison of poetry to numismatics is
precious information; it indicates to us, better than my
words could do, the idea that Voltaire had of Art. A
poetic work was for him an object of curiosity that
connoisseurs bent over, to look at through the magni-
fying glass, and the most cunning observer was the
one who discovered the most defects. He went out of
his way, proud of his good eyes, and scoffed at others. And there we have Voltaire's esthetic. He alone
who has the diploma of a connoisseur has the right to
shiver before a Laocoön group statue; and that is
quite clear. How else do you expect to feel the beauty
of a masterpiece if you are not a connoisseur in numismatics?

* * *

To be honest, I am almost ashamed to cite what

Voltaire had no shame in saying. However, one must continue:

> *One is afflicted when one considers, principally in cold and humid climates, that prodigious throng of men who haven't the least glimmer of taste, who love none of the beaux arts.*

If those unfortunate inhabitants of cold and humid climates loved at least a single one of the beaux arts while detesting the others, that would be a consolation; but alas! the coldness and humidity of their climes oblige those unfortunate people to detest them all, would that it were only numismatics!

Let's continue!

> *Enter a small town in the countryside, you will rarely find one or two book-stores. In provincial capitals, those that have Academies even, how rare is that taste for them!*

Voltaire is really cruel! He has snatched away from me one of my last illusions! I who thought that Academies were everywhere, that beauty reigns without contradiction!

If at least each town possessed many book-stores, the beatitude would begin this very instant. But, alas! how tough the times are, and how rare the bookstores!

* * *

I have just put before your eyes some of the marvels of the last century: we were reading together, in the *Philosophical Dictionary*, some rather curious entries, and even though I had not opened that famous book, which is admired but not read, to the most important page in it doubtless: we were looking for Voltaire's artistic theories, and I had not opened it to his catechism on the word "Art."

What, a distraction? How is it I did not go straight to the heart of the matter from the start?

Here is my excuse: *The word "Art" is not found in the Philosophical Dictionary.*

I checked ten times before I could believe it. I will probably check again. There are things for which the testimony of the eyes does not suffice. There is in the world a *Philosophical Dictionary* that does not accord a place for the word "Art."

For example, you will find "beaux arts," you will find "dramatic art," "*ars poetica*," you will find the application, but you will not find the principle; you will find the details, but you will not find the unity.

* * *

Let's listen to Voltaire speak about drama, or rather tragedy; for drama, he does not know anything about it. We are going to see how he, who does not study, judges in its essence the thing he speaks of. We are going to hear a blind man put boundaries on a country that he does not know, that he has not seen, even on the map. We are going to hear the rulings of a judge who does not know the laws, who does not know even if a law exists.

There are many races of men. Some, when faced with a work of art, open the book of eternal things, and descend as deeply as possible into their soul to find there some written judgment.

They think that real connoisseurs are those who know absolute truth best and the universal relationship of truths to themselves. Others think that art is a specialty, and that connoisseurs are those who have forgotten life, love, truth, in order to learn many rules by heart. Voltaire, who is at the head of that latter group, asks:

> *Where to find in our modern nations a metaphysician, a moralist even, who has spoken well of poetry? They are weighed down by the names of Homer, Virgil, Sophocles, Ariosto, and Tasso, and all those who have enchanted the earth with the harmonious productions of their genius. They have not felt the beauties contained in them, or, if they felt them, they would like to destroy them."*

You can see just how far, according to Voltaire, metaphysicians' hatred of Art goes. That assertion, by its bizarreness, deserves an explanation, which is refused to us. One of two things: either they do not have a feeling for the beauties of art, or, if they have a feeling for them, pressured by a singular and really inexplicable feeling, they would like to destroy them. As well, Voltaire, doubtless with the fear of committing one of those two crimes, keeps himself continually at an infinite distance from metaphysics. He is going to speak about dramatic art without having laid down the principles, willy-nilly, without a plan, without a theory, without discussion; he is going to bump up against, by chance, in his irregular promenade, the names of Shakespeare and Racine.

Because, for him, all art is tragedy. Shakespeare to him is a wild drunk, in whom he really wants to recognize, by force of indulgence, some qualities. Thus, he kills two birds with one stone: he makes the author of *Hamlet* ridiculous in the eyes of the French reader, and reserves for himself, Voltaire, the glory of apperceiving some flowers in that dung heap:

> *The Italians, the French, men of letters of every country who have not lived some time in England, take Shakespeare for a Gille of the country fair, for a clown lower than Harlequin, for the most contemptible buffoon who ever amused the populace.*

Happily, the author of *Mohamet* had lived for some time in England, and, thanks to that circumstance, he puts Shakespeare above Harlequin.

Suddenly Voltaire wonders what is the greatest of all works of art? Where to find it? In what tragedy necessarily, for he knows nothing else. And what will be the model for tragedy? That is the question.

> *It is, he says, so difficult an enterprise to assemble in the same place the heroes of antiquity, to make them speak in French verse, not to make them enter or exit the scene except by design; to make them speak a* continually charming *language that is neither pompous nor familiar, but such a work is a prodigy. One must observe finally the rules of poetry and those of the theater, which are nearly countless.*

An ignoramus playwright might substitute men for heroes at times, and he might give in perhaps to the temptation of making his characters speak like moderns and, from time to time, familiarly. But the well-apprised poet knows that it is absolutely necessary to assemble ancient heroes *in the same place*, and to condemn them to a *continually charming* language; and when he has fulfilled that harsh treatment, it still remains for him to observe all the rules of the theater, which are nearly innumerable! What would be that work of art, that prodigy, that will show us so many ancient heroes brought together in the same place?

> *Would it not be, says Voltaire,* Iphigenia in Aulis*?*

> *From the first line of verse, he adds, I feel myself interested and* touched. *My curiosity is excited by the single lines of verse that a simple officer of Agamemnon's speaks, harmonious verse, charming verse, verse as no other poet*

wrote them at that time.

Touched by the encounter between Arcas and Agamemnon, Voltaire forgets that the verses are Racine's; he is surprised *that a simple officer* could deliver such harmonious and charming verses.

A little later:

Before Racine, not only did nobody know the way of the heart, but almost nobody knew the finesses of versification. Nobody was familiar with that happy combination of long and short syllables, and consonants followed by vowels, which make verse flow with such softness, and which makes it enter the sensitive and just ear with such pleasure.

I will refrain from commenting on those exquisite phrases. Racine discovered the finesses of versification, the combination of long and short syllables, and the way of the heart to boot. I would make only one permissible remark, where it is a question of a fanatical grammarian: from the grammatical point of view, the last phrase makes no sense.

Voltaire continues:

One knows just how sublime the scene in the fourth act is, not the sublimeness of declamation, not the sublimeness of sought-after thoughts or gigantesque expressions, but that which a mother in despair has of the most pen-

> *etrating and most terrible kind, that*
> *which a young princess who feels her*
> *unhappiness has of the most touching*
> *and noble kind. Never has Achilles*
> *been more Achilles than in that piece.*

If that long phrase is not French, one has to blame the enthusiasm that side-tracked Voltaire at that very moment then; and, if that enthusiasm is a little cold, it is easy to explain that frigidity. Feeling gives way to the ideal. Its intensity is by virtue of the power that produces it. It is that conception of beauty that gives to the love of beauty its justice and its majesty. To admire, one must know. Admiration is the privilege of generalizing spirits. These latter alone rise from act to idea, and tap enthusiasm at the eternal source. Voltaire has analyzed *Iphigenia*.

Not only did he not resolve, but he did not raise, with respect to that tragedy, a single question. His admiration is distracted by the happy combination of long and short syllables. But the life of the drama, its idea, its intellectual and moral range, if there is one, those things do not even enter his mind. Whether his praises are merited or not, it does not matter much.

The essential matters have not been touched on. He counts the rules to see if the author hasn't forgotten one. He reads, caliper in hand, in order to measure the length of the scenes and those of the acts. He reads like an old professor. He admires in the name of conventional poetics and official rhetoric. He believes, as schoolboys believe in middle school, that it is the teacher who sets the conditions of success: he trudges around arbitrary things; but he does not approach any reality. For Art in his mind does not become one with life. It is not a living truth. The *noble* style, the entrances of individuals, their exits, etc. everything was taken into consideration in his analysis, except God, man, and nature.

* * *

Voltaire affirms that *Iphigenia in Aulis* is a perfect piece. Racine, without other comparison, is in his eyes the greatest poet in the world, but he accompanies those judgments with the following observation:

> *An ode that Racine composed at the age of eighteen for the marriage of the king earned him a present that he was not expecting,* and that decided him for poetry.

Racine would have been a public prosecutor or bailiff then, if Louis XIV hadn't by chance made him a gift; it is that gift that revealed to him his vocation. It is at that moment that he felt shivering inside himself the creative spirit. If Voltaire had known what he was talking about when he spoke about Art, he would have understood that that sovereign is too proud not to choose his servants himself. He does not wait for Louis XIV's gifts. He takes his men where he finds them; he consecrates them and that's it.

As for Corneille,

> *Cardinal Richelieu, having persecuted* The Cid, *had the good-naturedness to inspire in him that noble vexation and*

> *that generous obstinacy that made him*
> *compose his admirable scenes of* Ho-
> race *and* Cinna.

So it was the liking of gifts that inspired
Racine, and vexation that inspired Corneille. It is in
Voltaire's destiny and in his nature to demean whatever he touches, even if he had the intention of elevat-
ing it: his hands were not made for that.

There are two sorts of adversary, those who
pose the question as you do, but who resolve it in the
opposite sense, and those who do not pose it, who do
not know even that there is a question. With the first
sort, agreement can be difficult, but it is possible at a
pinch. With the second, agreement is absolutely impossible, as they do not understand the language you
speak. The same words do not awaken the same idea
in their mind and in yours. At the same moment, and
relative to the same word, Voltaire, believing that he
is thinking of Art, thinks of the tricks of the theater,
the intrigues in the wings, the entrances, the exits, the
rules that are innumerable. You and he, you have not
one single word to say to each other.

> *Fundamentally, asked Voltaire some-*
> *where, is genius anything other than*
> *talent?*

This is not the place for me to go on about the
radical difference between those two ideas. Genius
and talent do not differ by degree: they differ by nature. The man of genius is someone who exceeds the
proportions that man ascribes to man. When posterity
speaks about him, it does not always distinguish ex-

actly between the ideal and reality because in the man of genius the ideal and reality are more tightly caught up together than ordinarily. In the story of his life, history and legend solemnly rub elbows.

But a young woman has talent when she plays the piano agreeably.

Voltaire believes that the word that is appropriate for Christopher Columbus and the one that is appropriate for that young woman are synonymous.

I continue:

> *Taste, says Voltaire, that gift of discerning our aliments, has produced in all known languages the metaphor that expresses the feeling for beauties and defects in the arts with the same word. It is a prompt discernment like that of the tongue and palate, which informs, like it, reflection. The gourmand promptly feels and recognizes the mixture of two liqueurs. The man of taste, the connoisseur, will see, in an eye blink, the mixture of two styles.*

(Two liqueurs and two styles!)

But let's continue:

> *The man of taste will see a defect next to a charm.*

What is it, if you don't mind, that *charm* that can only be appreciated by the fine connoisseur? Here we go:

> *What would you expect that he should*
> *do against three? That he should die!*

But, says Voltaire, he will feel an involuntary disgust in the following line:

> *Or that a beautiful despair should pos-*
> *sess him at that moment.*

I am not sure whether Voltaire's disgust was voluntary or involuntary, and I do not examine that question. But the second line of verse would be as admirable as the first, if the adjective were removed.

> *A sensible young man will be moved,*
> *continues Voltaire, on the first repre-*
> *sentation of a fine tragedy; but he will*
> *distinguish in it neither the merit of*
> *the unities, nor that delicate art by*
> *which no individual either enters or*
> *exits without a reason, nor other sur-*
> *mounted difficulties.*

Poor young man! Not only will he not be a connoisseur, he will be incapable of feeling anything but beauty. But, admitted to the school of Voltaire, he will disentangle the merit of the unities, he will share in his master's incessant preoccupation with entrances and exits, and he will no longer admire in Art anything but surmounted difficulties! What progress!

> *One must, continues Voltaire, have a*
> *well-tuned mind to feel all the beauties*
> *in* Henriade.

And elsewhere:

> *One asks how poetry, being so little*
> *necessary in the world, occupies so*
> *high a place among the* beaux arts?
> *One can ask the same question about*
> *music.*

I do not comment, I cite. What might be my
reflections next to citations? Citations could fill vol-
umes: I find myself in the awkward situation of an
immense choice. But I stop there, thinking I have said
enough to show the conception that Voltaire has of
Art.

> *Taste, he says again somewhere, is*
> *shared among a very small number of*
> *people:* the entire populace *is exclud-*
> *ed. Taste, for the ordinary person, is*
> *not introduced except with opulent*
> *idleness.*

One last word: we have heard Voltaire insult
Plato. Let us hear him insult Pascal. You recognize
the great man's words.

> *Man is a reed, but a thinking reed; if*
> *the universe should crush him, man*
> *would still be nobler than what de-*
> *stroys him because the universe knows*
> *nothing about the advantage it has*
> *over him.*

Voltaire responds:

> *What does that word* "noble" *mean?*
> *It is quite true that my thought is*
> *something else altogether than, for ex-*

ample, the planet of the sun. But is it quite proven than an animal, because it has some thoughts, is nobler than the sun which animates all we know of in nature? Is it up to man to decide? He is judge and partisan. One says that one work is superior to another when it costs more trouble to its author and when it is more useful. But didn't it cost the Creator more to make the sun than to kneed together a small animal, five feet tall about, who reasons well or poorly? Which of the two is more useful to the world, that animal, or that star that shines on so many planets? And in what way are some ideas received in a brain preferable to a material universe?

There you have it, Voltaire's reasoning: How could thought be superior to matter, given that matter is grosser than thought?

The Ones and the Others

The man of genius is not someone who thinks, or who always thinks at any rate, about different things than other men do, but when he thinks about the same things, he thinks about them differently.

He thinks about them in their intimate reality. He thinks about numbers in their relationship to the whole. He can say what everyone else has said before him but say something absolutely new. How is that? It's his secret. The lion's paw leaves its imprint.

The man of genius and another man can both use the word Art; but the same word will not mean the same thing in both their mouths. The cedar and the grass blade receive the same light from the same sun, but they assimilate it differently.

He sees the same light as others, but he sees it from a particular angle. From that angle, the things that appear disunified to others appear unified to him, and his gaze approaches the very principle of liaison. He follows rivers from their source, to where they throw themselves into the same sea, and if he does not reach that latter place, he thinks about it and tends toward it.

He has for auxiliaries in this world the just mind and the simple mind.

The just mind, perceiving certain true relationships, respects and admires the man who, in the same direction, perceives others, more hidden, more distant. The simple mind respects, admires, and loves the man of genius, because genius is nothing more than the highest expression of human simplicity. Simplicity sees itself in genius as in a faithful mirror, but enlarging its object. Ordinary things grow bigger when genius touches them: the words that a genius uses express more than they tell. Genius, like lightning, exposes the horizon.

The man of genius has for his adversary the man of talent; for an enemy the man of wit; for a mortal enemy the mediocre man.

The man of talent denies him, the man of wit mocks him, the mediocre man tries to mock him given he cannot annihilate him.

The man of talent, satisfied with what he has, wants nothing from that rich man who, however, is found to be poor and who, giving more than any other man, still finds that he does not give anything. He does not believe that there is anywhere a sphere superior to that small sphere where he keeps himself, where he enjoys himself, where he amuses himself, where he amuses others.

The man of wit laughs because, not believing in surfaces, he pities the fool who wants to pierce them. When Christopher Columbus boards his ship, he laughs because he himself is not in the habit of leaving for America, and it is not impossible that he should receive some nice ribbing.

As for the mediocre man, his rage has a character apart, and one does not know it well except when one knows him well. It is at the bottom of his heart that he is wounded, and in order to sound the wound one must needs go to the bottom of that heart, which is deep in its way, like a void, like a hole.

He has no need to know even vaguely what the man of genius did, nor what he is about, in order to hate him. No; he is recognized by his signature, and he hates him, without knowing why, with an animal's hatred that that instinct gives to certain inferior beings. He hates him and he wants to harm him, in order to do something bad to something great. His vanity, which has much to avenge, aims at that, without even being conscious of it, like a universal vengeance, like a triumph that would indemnify everything. Also, he stirs up his nothingness in order to find something; he tries contempt even, impossible and aborted contempt: he succeeds only in exhaling revolting miasmas that would want to be poisons and that help to divine what exists in souls that have nothing in them.

The French Language

Who ever thought that a dictionary was a book?

It is a book that we should open sometimes. There are some more or less instructive ones. I open one by chance, by M. Dochez, to the article "Vanity."

The old meaning of the word is made clear to me very clearly by the old French:

> *"Vanity (from Latin* vanitas, *derived from* vanus, vide*): Things are said and believed in very madly, and are full of vanity and sovereign legerity or falsity." (RAOUL DE PRESLES.)*

It is clear that vanity means emptiness.

Now to the moderns:

> *"Vanity is nothing more than the art of putting on one's Sunday best every day."*

The phrase is Balzac's, and you were able to recognize him. There you have it, vanity, considered not in itself, in its essence, but from its exterior and social effect.

Let's continue:

> *"Vanity is the mother of ridicules like idleness is the mother of vices."*

You cannot guess the author's name: too many people are capable of signing their name to such sottishness. This one belongs to Marmontel: that good man believed that vanity is not the mother of vices, and that it is limited to producing absurdities.

Let's continue:

"What mortifying consequences the first impulses of vanity attract!"

Oh! who do we have here, but J.-J. Rousseau! The phrase is by him and must be by him. He condemns vanity doubtless, but in the name of what does he condemn it? He condemns it in the name of vanity itself. He engages you to defy him, because it has mortifying consequences, that is to say because it turns against itself, and it succeeds by showing itself to make itself suffer. Just like that, vanity, observed by itself, and condemned in its own name, not by virtue of error, but by virtue of poor calculation!

Let's continue:

"What makes the vanity of others insupportable to us is that it wounds our own."

You expect Larochefoucauld's signature, and you are not wrong. Here he is, the morose and, by consequence, limited observer, gifted by finesse and deprived of elevation, who observes in man only the defect, the absence, the lack, and who never sees in him any loving truth because he does not look high enough to perceive his loftiness.

Let's continue:

"Vanity loses them, pride would save

them."

It is to Mme. de Girardin that that phrase must be imputed. She believed, alas! that pride is a noble thing that can save someone, and proved to us that she was not speaking the language of truth. She was wishing to be witty, and she proved to us that she was ignorant of, in their relationship, the two words she pits against each other.

Let's continue:

"Vanity is so anchored in a man's heart that a churl, a kitchen hand, a picklock boasts and wants to have admirers." (PASCAL.)

Things are starting to improve, and yet nothing has been said really.

Pascal is mistakenly surprised, if he is even surprised. What is there to be surprised about in a churl, a kitchen hand, a picklock wishing to have admirers any more than anyone else? A picklock is a man, and vanity is no more ridiculous or vicious in him, because of his condition, which is only a detail, than in any other person. If Pascal is not surprised, he allows at least his reader to be surprised, and that is already too much. Pascal thus flatters the vanity of his reader, who is not a picklock but who is a man.

I omit a large number of citations and I come to what will terminate the article.

"How human vanity must blush to see the fatal term that divine Providence

has given to its false hopes."

And that is Bossuet: that much is clear: do you not detect the lion claw?

M. Dochez kept that citation for last, as a conclusion. It is not by chance: it is an intelligent and oft-used practice that pervades the entire work.

After having escorted us through the history of words, following the contours and detours of the language, the author keeps for the end of the article the concluding citation, which summarizes and decides. He wants that the literary history of our national genius should have a conclusion. I recall how, in the last years of his life, chatting with me about the French language that he so loved, and putting everything that he wanted to cite in his work in the best light, M. Dochez often said to me: "I would like my Dictionary to be useful to a young man, even in order for him to become a Christian. I would like the reader to understand that the true sense of things is taught by Christianity. I would like the Christian conclusion to be visible at the end of each article. I would not," he added, with charming scruple, "like to make the name of those who lied be loved."

There we have it, a most certainly novel and lofty manner in which to conceive of a dictionary! There we have it, a philosophical dictionary in an acceptation of those two words that are not commonly employed together!

M. Dochez did not live long enough to see that work, which he had devoted his life to, printed and published. Death took him from the knowledge of it and from his friends, when the last pages of his book were still at the press.

A member of the Institute, whose authority is considerable in linguistic matters, M. Paulin Paris, in a learned preface, gave homage to that learned author.

M. Paulin Paris perfectly understood and explained the kind of service that M. Dochez had done for the French language. Here are some words that I would like to cite:

> *It is not easy, he says, to follow the French language from its origin, in its transformations, through the numerous incidents of its history. Also, despite the attraction that philological research presents, one has never studied it in a general, absolute fashion. It is not that we lack good vocabularies or recommendable grammarians...*
>
> *But all those habile critics esteem the value of words according to their taste, or at least they are content to invoke, in support of their judgments, recent and so-to-speak immediate examples... It is unusual if, in their decisions, they recognize the influence of social revolutions, and if they really want to record what terrains, previously gone over, have borne new elements and unexpected nuances into the waves that wash before our eyes.*

> *According to them, the history of our*
> *language would have started in the*
> *reign of François 1ˢᵗ... Did not Vol-*
> *taire believe he discovered that we*
> *babble a jargon, a half-breed formed*
> *of Goths and Normands?... We lack a*
> *work that has gone into sufficient*
> *depth into the origin of consecrated*
> *words, into the date of their introduc-*
> *tion, into their divers acceptations,*
> *into the idea they suggested formerly,*
> *and into the idea they express today. It*
> *is a work of that nature that the re-*
> *spectable and learned M. Dochez had*
> *undertaken in his laborious retreat,*
> *and today we present it to the public.*

That preliminary discourse is itself a curious and precious monument. M. Paulin Paris speaks to us on our origins like a man familiar with them. He clarifies what can be called the first epoch of French literature. The minstrels, modern rhapsodists of a sort, were our first poets really. An oral tradition alone, very incomplete, preserved their songs until Philippe-Auguste's contemporary copiests captured them, but who, as M. Paulin Paris quite well knows, did not provide their exact date. In that first epoch, epoch of knights and villeins, the nation did not know how to read.

In the second epoch, written literature begins. Now we find ourselves under Philippe-Auguste. One takes the art of writing seriously. A companion of Godefroi de Bouillon, Richard le Pèlerin, had composed, in the twelfth century, under this title, *le Geste d'Antioche*, a tale of the first crusade.

One hundred years later, still in the second epoch, a trouvère from Douai rejuvenated that work according to the already more learned rules of the thirteenth century. Already the naïvety was lost, already in the thirteenth century! Whoever could have seen, with a penetrating eye, the birth of the Alexandrine, could have predicted the seventeenth century.

Those poetic attempts are succeeded by stories, and the personality of the French language develops appreciably. French prose had an earlier and fuller existence than poetry; Jean Froissart is there to attest to it; and it is easy to grasp in him that particular charm that no longer permits renouncing either a language or a man.

M. Dochez's book brings back those titles of nobility to the French language.

We do not know enough about our language, we do not love it enough. It is our veritable expression, and what better way to dignantly glorify France? To study our language, one must study our history, and to study our history one must study our mission, our type, our destiny, our place and function in the history of the world. Now, if I'm not mistaken, this is the character, the double character of France. It is essentially one with humanity, and essentially distinct from other nations. By its roots, it digs into the entire world; by its head, by its fruits, by its flowers, it resembles only itself. It takes its good where it finds it, and never does it plagiarize: for it assimilates all that it borrows.

It seizes the Latin element, it seizes the German element, it conserves the Gallic element, and it is France. Always ready to help others, but always faithful to itself; there it is, I believe, the character that France must have, in its history. Its type is equally distant from egoism and imitation, and I would summarize its portrait by these two phrases: Essentially bound in solidarity, essentially personal.

What is true of France is true of the French language. The French language is to expression what France is to action. France is personal, the French language possesses its originality; France is bound by solidarity, the French language possesses a marvelous faculty of assimilation.

Ah! if it was reduced to what one calls the Gallic spirit, it would occupy, on the map of the intellectual world, quite a small place. But see how prepared it is for all aggrandizement. It bends for everything, but never loses its shape. Even though it might not be familiar naturally with great philosophical conceptions, even though they do not seem to it to be a product of the sun, it accepts them with admirable facility, it assimilates them, it makes them its own. And when it makes them its own, it has the admirable power of disseminating them over the earth. The French language has the gift of popularizing!

Sublime or dangerous faculty! At once both clear and subtle, the French language can vulgarize the true or false thoughts of a solitary; it can present under a delicate form, salutary one moment and per-

fidious the next, depending on the occasion, the sentiments that, without it, would seem abrupt and, thereby, lose their effect on the human heart. The originality of the allure and the suppleness of the movements
will everywhere distinguish France and the French
language, distinguish them from other nations, other
languages, and at the same time unite them. Resem-
bling nothing, but assimilating everything, that there
perhaps is the secret of conquest, and the reason for
victory. When Bossuet makes use of Saint Augustine,
he does not translate him servilely, he becomes nourished by him, and remains Bossuet, armed with his
conquest.

Thoughts

Suppose two men, otherwise equal by the faculties until now deposited in them, but reawakened this morning with the following dispositions:

One of the two, who calls himself Jacques, rises today just as he rose yesterday, the day before, the day before that, last week, last month, and last year.

That man does not say his prayers on rising, because he is not in the habit of saying them, or if he is in the habit by chance, then he says them by habit, and when pronouncing this phrase – "Hallowed be thy name," – he does not ask himself whether it means anything or not.

That man gets bored, just as he got bored yesterday, without even realizing he was getting bored! If someone points it out to him, he responds: "What do you want!"

He is resigned to eternal boredom.

His day today will have no more reason for being than the day before.

The other man, whom I have just supposed (we will call him, if you like, Etienne), admits the possibility of a change, any change, in his person and in his life.

One could believe that this is a small thing.

On waking, Etienne did not declare to himself that he is immutable, infallible, and perfect. Etienne did not say to himself: I am perfection, therefore I have only to keep on keeping on, to resemble myself, to imitate myself. Etienne has admitted the idea of a modification as not being incompatible with the idea of himself.

Really, that seemed simple and facile.

Eh well! that is an effort, that is great, that is beautiful.

That is unimaginably fecund.

Etienne has begun to waver. We see him in route, he is moving in the direction of life.

As for Jacques, who did not say anything to himself this morning, – by the very fact that he did not say anything to himself, he said what is implied by that: "Let's keep going. I will do what I have always done." He is going to sojourn another day in death, to get used to it one more day, to strengthen the bonds that unite him to it; his friendship with death is going to become more intimate; for a day is a respectable and important thing.

Between morning and evening man travels a great deal, sometimes to the right, other times to the left.

Now, of Jacques who does what he has always done, or Etienne who thinks he is doing what he needs to do – who is right?

Because a mistake has already been made, is that sufficient reason to repeat the mistake, to repeat it forever?

My question is stupid, because it is easy to resolve. At the moment I posed it, you resolved it theoretically, without hesitation, in favor of Etienne. But please ask yourself whether earlier this morning you would have actually resolved it in Jacques' favor.

* * *

To be right among imbeciles, requires a gentle and smooth touch. The lie, which is in general polished, courteous, smooth-tongued and sweetened, appears moderate to them. The simple touch, energetic and sometimes brusk, but in good faith, displeases them, shocks them, upsets them.

* * *

Wicked men know how to weep at the right moment.

* * *

The mediocre man, when one points out a great danger to him which he had not thought of before, responds: "*Ah bah!*" or "*Come on!*" The accident that you speak to him about, not being something he's accustomed to, for the mediocre man, he is convinced that it cannot happen, given that it has not happened to him before.

* * *

The ardor of seeing superior men, or those who pass for such, is, with a young man, an almost certain mark of intelligence; that ardor is one of the manifestations of his need to interrogate. Sots do not like new faces. They are too satisfied with themselves to have need for someone or something else.

* * *

The mediocre man, bothered by the superior man's look, takes refuge in mockery, like an asylum.

* * *

One must be strong and even great to be the first to call a man or thing by its true name.

* * *

When a man deceives you, you should tell yourself that had he been committed to sharing some knowledge with you, he would not have done as much. A single betrayal by a friend instructs much more than ten years of hard work by the same.

* * *

It is the exclusive characteristic of false situations to be complicated by all the effort one makes to clarify them. Complicated by speech, complicated by silence, they always get muddled up, no matter what one does or does not do. But if someone said: *I was wrong, forgive me*, that is all it takes to shed some light on all that chaos.

* * *

A man who has done you wrong and who regrets it, tries a hundred thousand complicated, difficult, and pointless ways to get out of an embarrassing situation. But to repair his mistake and say: *I made a mistake*, that would be too simple, too prompt, too efficacious; he does not think of it.

* * *

Something deferred is not lost. A true phrase sometimes, true even in principle. But, in the relative scheme of things, the misuse one does with it is redoubtable. How many things have been irretrievably lost for not having been acted on at the right moment! Opportunity is one of the favors that time accords us, and here is one of the most terrible expressions in the human language: *Too late!*

* * *

That man is irritated with his father: he is going to fail in his filial duties. All of a sudden a thought runs through his head: one day his father will die. One day my father will be dead, one day I will go to the cemetery, and I will read his name on a tomb. I will remember then the trouble I am about to cause him. What an extraordinary glimmer of light death casts on life!

* * *

Be wary of the man who seeks to make his qualities stand out in your presence.

* * *

Partiality for the weak and vanquished is the injustice of superior souls.

* * *

Few men speak with the same tone of voice to someone they have need of and someone who has need of them.

* * *

Affection fills the abysses. Place an ordinary, but devoted man next to a good man, the first will be in one
sense equal to the second, and sometimes, on stormy
days, his superior.

* * *

Looking for oneself leads to all kinds of complica-
tions, leads to all sorts of labyrinths. Abandonment of
oneself simplifies everything.

* * *

When a man gets lost, you can be sure that he had just
gone looking for himself.

* * *

When we hear a man speak, who is free of any taint
of self-love, we put an extraordinary confidence in his
words, in spite of ourselves even.

* * *

Once a man has just lost himself, by one of those mistakes that is also called stupidities, because they lead
to an immediate punition, do not ask why he got lost:
you can be sure that it was on account of self-love.

* * *

Self-love undermines and divides. Some people believe that one must excite the vanity of young men, so
that they might turn self-love to their advantage. One
would do better to lace a glass of water with arsenic,
to give it more taste.

* * *

Self-love blinds those who love the light, paralyzes those who love action, perverts those who love goodness, makes those who love intelligence stupid. Buildings that once towered, crumble when self-love slips in through a crack between two stones. Self-love is essentially contrary to edification.

* * *

Nothing remains healthy where self-love appears. It covers and sullies everything like leprosy. It empoisons the bone marrow, and the bones decay.

* * *

The look that a man casts on himself so as to admire himself sparks lightning. The look that a man casts on himself so as to know himself and confound himself disposes the lightning to go out.

* * *

No natural quality substitutes for common sense. Without it, the highest faculties serve merely to dig the abyss that surrounds you and threatens you. The more elevated you are, the deeper the abyss. Great endeavors, when common sense is lacking, prepare only for great ruin.

* * *

One needs courage to believe and audacity to doubt.

* * *

The man who, for his own fault, missed a great opportunity would like to make believe that he pitied those who did not miss it like he did.

* * *

The man who has betrayed a secret, instead of blaming himself, blames the secret.

* * *

The man who has betrayed his friend tells himself three things to reassure himself: to start, that his friend deserved to be betrayed; then, that his friend had an interest in being betrayed; finally, that his friend has not really been betrayed at all.

After some time, he has persuaded himself that there had been nothing but a misunderstanding in all that business. Several days later he is happy with himself and says that he did right.

* * *

At solemn moments when a man basks in full light, in a feeling of infinity, if he experiences a need for silence; it is not because he has nothing to say, but because he would have everything to say; it is not the object that lacks speech, it is speech that lacks an object. He is afraid to employ words that are also called terms, and to circumscribe and annihilate, by describing it, the immense and timid joy that rises from the bottom of his soul, and hovers over the world, without landing on it, feeling that it is too small. He is afraid to snuff out the flame if it imprisons him; he is afraid to fall back into slavery at the very instant when he would try to express the inexpressible and to tell of his deliverance.

Reputation and Glory

Two routes are available to the man who speaks to other men. In supposing success, those two routes end, the one in reputation, the other in glory.

What do those two words represent? What is the distance that separates reputation and glory?

The blindest people sense that the distance is great, without knowing what it consists of: instinctively man is obliged not to confound them: the tongue refuses to accept confusion. Who then would dare speak about the reputation of Saint Augustine, or the glory of Helvetius?

Reputation therefore is not glory. But one generally believes that there exists between those two a difference of degree, and that reputation would have only to grow a little in order to turn into glory. That there is the error. The difference that exists between them is a difference of nature. Reputation is a parody and the opposite of glory.

Art is the expression of the ideal manifested in a perceptible sign. It has for an evident goal, for a natural end, to elevate towards the ideal whomever approaches that perceptible sign. But the artist has fallen because the man is demeaned; and the artist, full of his decline, full of emptiness, full of vanity, forgetting that his task is to elevate men to it, that is to say to the ideal that he expresses, consents to lower himself to men, not in order to lure them by it up to the heights, but to remain with them down in the depths. So that instead of looking for the law of art in eternal law and in absolute truth, he has sought his law in the public's caprice. Instead of striving to elevate men, he has chosen to please them. The artist seeks to please! what appalling degradation! Every habitude that we have of *extraordinary* things is needed in order not to be surprised by that complaisance.

The artist who flatters the public strives for reputation.

The artist who elevates the public strives for glory.

Glory comes from on high, reputation from below.

Glory is the resplendence that truth places on the brow of the man it has chosen. Glory is the reflection of God, to whom alone it belongs exclusively and essentially.

Reputation is the work of advertising.

The light does not preside over its birth.

It often forms and grows by manœuvres, machinations, intrigues; it knows subterranean ways.

Reputation follows the current of received opinions; glory goes against the current.

Reputation advances in a spiral and slithers like a serpent on the ground, it crawls in order to insinuate itself; glory flies in the sky, and its flight is a battle, for the earth does not love to be dominated: it furnishes the lead shot in order to kill birds.

The theater of glory is the invisible world. Success has nothing to do with it.

The reputation that starts out causes your rivals to talk about you and to say among themselves: Watch out, here comes another one!

The glory that starts out leaves those whom it will upset in an absolute exterior calm. It has nothing menacing about it, at least not in appearance, for anyone. Its resources being non-existent, its enemies think that it is going to die, without their needing to bother themselves to kill it; they oppose to it a particular kind of disdain, that disdain of rich mediocrity, which says, while looking at genius: *I have more money than you do, and my place is already set.*

And nevertheless the mustard grain germinates and grows. Its enemies' disquietude will begin soon enough; the first shimmerings of the sun that is about to rise bother them in their sleep, and they have a nightmare.

A nascent reputation creates in the newly-made man's rivals a certain exterior disquieted, but it is small and mediocre, like the situation: they sense merely a rival. A nascent glory creates in those who look on, an absolute exterior tranquility, for the means of success are null; but if they looked deep inside themselves (one would need, for that to happen, to stop being mediocre), they would find there a strange fright, of a different order, which they cannot put a name on, and which they would not wish to speak about: that would be the feeling of their next defeat, and if that mute feeling was obliged to let out a cry, it would cry this: "Behold my conqueror." That attitude of mediocrity in the face of genius is one of the saddest and happiest spectacles on earth.

Reputation is founded on known bases; its progress is appreciable. It advances prudently and calculates all its steps; then, after it has calculated well, it perceives that it miscalculated. It almost always misses the goal it was aiming for and arrives often, at old age, in an obscurity that is a punition.

Glory is born in another kind of obscurity, the obscurity of initiation; it leaves just as it came, without knowing why. Then it continues to grow and attains the end without having aimed for it.

In the life and progress of reputation, everything is calculation.

In the life and progress of glory, everything is mystery.

Glory leads its own to the left whereas reputation wants them to come on the right.

Mediocre men who have made a reputation for themselves always propose, in order to manage the affairs of this world, arrangements of an apparent clarity, which resemble the common sense of inferior, limpid men, accessible to every intelligence, easy to grasp, presenting at first glance a resemblance to the evidence. Those arrangements have only one defect, which is not to account for mystery, which is behind everything. Their arrangements do not surpass the sphere of probabilities. Also, they are thwarted by that minister of God who is called the unexpected, and who is the visible representative of mystery.

Men can make a man's reputation; they cannot make his glory. Reputation is prepared; glory bursts out. Reputation is made by such and such a means; glory has no means at its service: it is, or it is not, like life. Reputation shines, glory resplends. Hability can lead to reputation; nothing leads to glory, except him who directs his eagles' gaze at the sun.

When a man has made his reputation, he can find again, in the sand, the traces of his steps that led him to where he has come, and his friends try to follow him by marching as he marched.

When glory shines on a man, no one can follow, on any geographical map, the route that the aureole took to find his face.

To make oneself a reputation, one must have many things, many instruments, many procedures.

To be born for glory, there is but one means, and that is to be born; and, in general, God closes all the routes to reputation for a long time, if he has decreed glory for you.

He lets the rocket trace its almost invisible trajectory in the air, then, when he has brought it very high into the sky, he makes it burst in the middle of the darkness, and heads turn around to see the light.

Reputation begins amidst noise, glory in silence; reputation works things out amidst pleasure, glory prepares itself in tears.

Men of glory are perhaps those who, feeling

the human person to be inferior to their destinies, abandon themselves to the Spirit that blows, more confident in it than in themselves; those there are wise enough to know that their wisdom does not suffice to lead them, and they lend their hands to the invisible wisdom that conspires with great men to accomplish great things by them.

God lets reputations make themselves while He sleeps.

When he awakens, he makes glories appear.

Glory has the sun for a natural symbol. And nevertheless it obeys, in its development, the law of the mustard grain.

Reputations resemble those cries, empty of meaning, let out in the middle of the night, in pitch darkness, by drunkards who fight and disagree.

Glory has the cachet of unity. Every glory represents one idea. Reputation is the work of a multiple.[13] The man with a reputation does not represent any one idea, but, in general, some poorly understood interests. He has won his place, not by one act, but by many steps, which will not leave any luminous wake behind him in history.

Glory is the dominion of the eagle. Reputations' domain is the dung field, where insects, symbols of putrefaction, wallow, struggle, devour each other.

---

[13]multiple: in the mathematical sense.

Conclusion

THE NINETEENTH CENTURY

Several years ago, if you declared that you were not Boileau's serf, you were enlisted, whether you liked it or not; and by the sole fact of your not accepting the rules of poetic Art, you were enlisted as one of Victor Hugo's serfs. If you did not admire, without restriction, Hugo's preface to *Cromwell*,[14] the reciprocal threatened you: you were enlisted among the serfs of poetic Art. Like the drunken peasant that Germans speak of, one had to fall to either the right or left. Few men understood the claim of standing up straight, even less that of genuflecting before the Truth that Is.

Now those old errors are nearly forgotten: they have not been replaced; they were abolished, but not corrected. The sounds of *Charivari* are nearly extinct. Harmony has not yet spoken.

If I cast a glance at the present situation of the moral world, if I want to sum up in a word the nineteenth century, considered from a natural point of view, I would say this: humanity wants to make its style.

Forced by the inertia of mechanical habits, human speech has rarely been the expression of man thus far.

Sometimes it has been an artifice directed by

---

[14]preface to *Cromwell*: Victor Hugo's preface to *Cromwell*, a Romantic drama published in 1827, was a kind of manifesto of art and style.

certain arbitrary conventions, and behold the literature that has been called classical.

That literature played at beauty.

Considering itself as a regular industry, it considered beauty its product.

Sometimes human speech has been a revolt, as infantile as its anterior slavery, and behold the literature that one calls Romantic.

With a hatred for the mechanical beauty that it wanted to topple, and in ignorance of where it was in terms of organic beauty, that literature wanted to place ugliness on the throne of art.

Considering itself a disheveled industry, Romanticism considered disorder to be its product.

Bound to one or the other of those two errors, the artist, to be able to work, stepped back from the general laws of life that ruled over him in his capacity as a man in order to subject himself to certain particular conventions, fabricated arbitrarily, that governed him as an artist.

The artist did not obey the same truth as man.

Such and such an artist did not obey the same truth as such and such another artist.

The lyrical poet and the satirical poet were strangers to one another, governed by absolutely different rules; for the division of genres, counterfeit of the truth, which belongs to speech, multiplied the rules, instead of only presenting the varied aspects of the laws.

Now, the tendency of humanity, in the nineteenth century, is to obey the same truths entirely.

The scholar turns to the artist, and the artist to the scholar: they each say to the other: "My brother."

The scholar and the artist turn toward man and they say to him: "My brother."

The scholar, the artist, and man turn toward God, and they have need of saying: "My Father."

However, those actions are not taken. We are still at the aspirations of them, we are not yet at the acts.

But the tendency exists.

Science, art, and life aspire to develop, each potency protecting its domains, under the empire of the same truth.

Separated by thought and by life, the words man spoke were not the man's style, they were the rhetor's style.

Reconciled with thought and life, at least insofar as this world is concerned, human speech will become man's style. For, I will say it again, here is the law: Man must

Live in truth,

Think as he lives,

Speak as he thinks.

That truth appears simple, and is simple, in effect, in its expression.

No one knows to what point that truth would be sublime, even in its imperfect realization.

Humanity has cut into and ruined the physical world; it has thereby prepared its style; speech didn't do it.

It must make a great effort, of splendor, faithfulness, simplicity, and love. It must take a great step towards the bottom of its heart; and from the bottom of its heart speech will rise up.

On the day that humanity takes control of its style, the intellectual face of the world will be changed.

Other Books by the Publisher

Fanchette's Pretty Little Foot
by Restif de La Bretonne

Je M'Accuse...
by Léon Bloy

My Hospitals & My Prisons
by Paul Verlaine

Salvation Through the Jews
by Léon Bloy

Words of a Demolitions Contractor
by Léon Bloy

Cellulely
by Paul Verlaine

Flowers of Bitumen
by Émile Goudeau

Songs for Her & Odes in Her Honor
by Paul Verlaine

On Huysmans' Tomb
by Léon Bloy

Ten Years a Bohemian
by Émile Goudeau

The Soul of Napoleon
by Léon Bloy

Other Books by the Publisher (cont.)

Blood of the Poor
by Léon Bloy

Theresa the Philosopher &
The Carmelite Extern Nun
by Marquis d'Argens &
Anne-Gabriel Meusnier de Querlon

A Platonic Love
by Paul Alexis

Two Novellas: Francine Cloarec's Funeral
and Benjamin Rozes
by Léon Hennique

The Revealer of the Globe: Christopher Columbus
& His Future Beatification (Part One)
by Léon Bloy

Joan of Arc and Germany
by Léon Bloy

Héloïse Pajadou's Calvary
by Lucien Descaves

An Immodest Proposal
by Dr. Helmut Schleppend

The Pornographer
by Restif de La Bretonne